The December Project

Also by Sara Davidson

*Joan: Forty Years of Life, Loss, and Friendship
with Joan Didion*

LEAP: What Will We Do with the Rest of Our Lives?

Cowboy

Loose Change: Three Women of the Sixties

Rock Hudson: His Story

Friends of the Opposite Sex

Real Property

The December Project

An Extraordinary Rabbi and a Skeptical Seeker
Confront Life's Greatest Mystery

SARA DAVIDSON

HarperOne
An Imprint of HarperCollinsPublishers

HarperOne

HarperCollins books may be purchased for educational, business, or sales promotional use. For information, please e-mail the Special Markets Department at SPsales@harpercollins.com.

HarperCollins website: http://www.harpercollins.com

HarperCollins®, ■ ®, and HarperOne™ are trademarks of Harper-Collins Publishers.

FIRST EDITION

Library of Congress Cataloging-in-Publication Data is available upon request.

ISBN 978-0-06-228174-6

14 15 16 17 18 RRD(H) 10 9 8 7 6 5 4 3 2 1

For my sister, Terry

Contents

Exercises

Preface

This is the story of a rabbi, a skeptical seeker, and the conversations we had about what we came to call the December Project. It began in 2009, when I was surprised by a call from Rabbi Zalman Schachter-Shalomi, the iconic storyteller, philosopher, and founder of the Jewish Renewal movement. We'd met many years before, and he knew I was a seeker who owned a doubting mind. My heart wanted to travel any road that might lead to truth or transformation, and my mind would come along and point out cracks in the paving.

At eighty-five, Reb Zalman proposed that we have a series of talks about what it's like "when you're in the December of your years and you know you're coming to the end of your tour of duty. What is the spiritual work of this time, and how do you prepare for the mystery?"

I jumped at the opportunity. I rarely found myself confronting the reality that one day I would cease to exist, and when I did, having no strong sense of an afterlife, I felt petrified. We began meeting every Friday and continued for two years, during which both of us were pushed up against the rock face. I went to Afghanistan and missed, by a few days, being killed by a suicide bomb. Reb Zalman struggled with a decline in health that was steeper than he'd expected. He created strategies to deal with pain and memory loss, and found tools to cultivate simplicity and joy. The tools and strategies, I realized, could be valuable at any stage of life. They were lessons for all our years, and I've included them as exercises you can try at the end of the book.

Throughout the story, I've placed sketches from Reb Zalman's life that illumine how he acquired his unique voice and insights. He was present at major flash points of the last century. He fled the Nazis in Austria, became an Orthodox rabbi in Brooklyn, landed in San Francisco at the height of the sexual revolution, and took LSD with Timothy Leary. He laid the foundation for a new denomination, Jewish Renewal, which encourages people to have a direct experience of God, and has influenced other Jewish groups as well as other faiths. He translated ancient prayers into contemporary language and helped make the religion accessible to secular people. He formed friendships with Thomas Merton and the Dalai Lama, was made an honorary sheikh in the Sufi order, and ended his career holding the World Wisdom Chair at a Buddhist university. All those threads are woven into what he brings to the December years.

I knew at the outset that my talks with Reb Zalman would be nourishing and provocative. The rabbi's omnivorous curiosity and jesting are infectious, and I hoped that exploring the movement of time through our lives would quicken my ability to relish every day. What I didn't anticipate was that our conversations would lead to a sea change in the way I face what we all must face, regardless of our beliefs or nonbelief: mortality.

The December Project

I Want to Loosen Your Mind

Midway through my sixties, I woke up in the middle of a June night and saw a comet streaking across a black sky. Bolting up in bed, I watched the fiery orb shoot from left to right, tracing the last third of a rainbow-like arc. It was not a dream—my eyes were open and everything else in my bedroom appeared as it normally does. Except for the comet. Was it a hallucination, a projection, a fragment of a dream leaking into my waking mind? I couldn't tell, but as I watched it burn down and disappear, I knew: that comet is your life, babe, and it's coming to the end of its trajectory. Are you spending your days the way you want to? A response rumbled up from deep within: NO.

In that season—the autumn of life—I was spending the majority of my hours in front of the computer. Most nights, I would have to forcibly push myself up from the desk chair to go to sleep. In the morning, the first thing I did was walk, still wearing my nightgown, to the computer and check e-mail. I had too many balls in the air, too many items on a list that never grew shorter, too much busyness and too little being accomplished. I wanted to play music, have a more robust social life, mentor young people, spend more time in nature, and connect with a man who could be a full partner. I was, instead, having a long-distance relationship with someone who measured out our time together with coffee spoons.

I fell back asleep, consoled by the thought that the next morning was my regular Friday visit with Reb Zalman. We'd been meeting for a year, since he'd asked me to discuss the stage of life he calls December, "when you can feel your cells getting tired, and your hard drive is running slow. I've been in your years, but you haven't been in mine, and I want to help people not freak out about dying."

That was intriguing—I certainly needed help in the almost impossible task of accepting in your bones that you're going to die. I understood that getting "up close with mortality," as Reb Zalman puts it, enables you to have a more heightened and grateful life, but at the time he invited me to have these talks, I was not looking death square in the eye. I was more concerned with how best to live whatever years were still ahead . . . to the very last drop.

I would have seized any excuse, though, to spend time with Reb Zalman. He's constantly deluged with requests for his blessings and counsel—for a family issue, spiritual crisis, or solace with a fatal illness. His insights generally come from an unexpected angle, and more important, he says, "the time I spend with people tastes good; it gives them endorphins. There's a carry-away of love, and if that's not there it won't work."

What I find unique about Reb Zalman is that he bridges two worlds—the ancient Orthodox and the current cutting edge. Born in Poland and ordained a Hasidic rabbi in Brooklyn, he has long been a trailblazer for individuals from many faiths. He's been a catalyst for the tectonic shift that began in the 1960s, moving away from what Zalman calls triumphalism—the belief that one religion is the best and only way—toward universalism, the recognition that, in Gandhi's words, "It is of no consequence by what name we call God in our homes."

Although he's tethered to the deepest roots of Judaism, Reb Zalman has not followed convention. He's been married four times and has eleven children, including one for whom he was a sperm donor to a lesbian rabbi. His life mission has been "to take the blinders off Judaism." Starting as a teen, he read psychology and philosophy books that were forbidden in his yeshiva, later communed with leaders of other faiths, and took mind-expanding drugs. He founded Jewish Renewal to help keep the tradition impassioned and alive, and he's ordained almost two hundred rabbis and cantors, who lead communities around the world. Every year when *Newsweek* compiles its list of the fifty most influential rabbis in America, Reb Zalman is on it.

Tall and striking in his younger years, Zalman is no less magnetic in his eighties. Each time I visit him, what I notice first are his eyes. Large and dark brown behind red tortoiseshell glasses, they meet you directly, saying, "You! You are the one I want to speak with now." When he smiles, there are glints in his eyes that signal his amusement and eagerness to be surprised. He's game to try new things, quick to adopt emerging technology, and reluctant to dismiss even the most outlandish idea. At seventy-nine, he tried hang gliding and started studying Arabic so his mind "wouldn't get stale," which spurred others to say, "He's the model of how I want to be when I'm older."

When we began meeting every Friday morning, it seemed accidental that we'd come together for this project. I was between books, treading water, at the very time he was seeking someone who could help him articulate what he was experiencing in December. If I wrote about our talks, he felt, his learning would be "uploaded" and "saved."

Before long, though, it did not seem random. After my close escape from the bombings in Kabul, my mother died of Alzheimer's. Both her parents had had dementia, and I worried I was heading for the same port. My youngest child got married, and an illness bearing the poetically apt name "labyrinthitis" brought my body to a stop, forcing me to reset my course and reach a dramatically different understanding of death.

Reb Zalman had to face a steady stream of health problems. He felt comfortable about his life ending but grew anxious and depressed when he couldn't walk well or catch his breath. He took every measure he could—seeing batteries of doctors and unorthodox healers—to keep his body going.

What made our talks zesty and unpredictable were the differences between us. I was raised Jewish, but the 613 commandments and all-powerful Hebrew God do not resonate with me as much as do the philosophies of Buddhism and Hinduism. For Reb Zalman, despite his rebelliousness and breaking of ground, Judaism is his oxygen and lifeblood. He welcomes the Sabbath by writing a note of love and gratitude to his wife, Eve Ilsen, which he slips under her dinner plate before she lights the candles and he blesses the wine. For the next twenty-four hours he does not travel, talk on the phone, or use the Internet, creating a sacred interlude separated from the rest of the week. I admire the practice of Shabbat but have never been moved to create it for myself.

Our meetings, though, became a ritual. At ten in the morning, I would drive to his home in Boulder, Colorado, at the base of the Flatirons—gray, triangular-shaped mountains jutting out over fields that, depending on the season, are covered with snow or ablaze with wildflowers. I'd ring the bell to let him know I'd arrived, then open the front door, which was rarely locked. Removing my shoes, I'd walk down to the basement, which is Reb Zalman's domain: a warren of dark rooms for praying, working, and meeting people. The rooms feel jumbled and chaotic, containing everything from an electric organ and a treadmill to portraits of rabbis going back generations, Hebrew prayer flags, shelves of books, tapes, DVDs and CDs, and an astonishing amount of techno clutter: computers, giant screens, numerous phones, a video camera, tripod, lights, a dozen voice recorders, and wires running in every direction.

On one of our first visits, he called, "I'll be right with you, Saraleh," when he heard me coming down the stairs. It was July 2009, the temperature was about to hit ninety, and Reb Zalman shuffled out from his computer room wearing slip-on sandals, knee-length shorts held up by suspenders, a short-sleeved black shirt unbuttoned at the neck, and a black knit yarmulke over his ample white hair. He opened his arms to hug me, then sat down in a reclining chair and I sat across from him, balancing my computer on my lap.

I asked how he was feeling.

"Thank God, my body's in pretty good shape right now," he said in his rich baritone, rapping his knuckles on the wooden arm of the chair. "I never dreamed I'd live this long. I've still got some mileage left, but the end is getting closer. I can hear the footsteps."

"Are you reconciled with that?" I asked, reminding him that in his book *From Age-ing to Sage-ing*, which he wrote in his sixties, he talked about his fear of being reduced to "a rocking-chair existence . . . and the eventual dark and inevitable end to my life."

"The rocking chair doesn't frighten me now," he said. "When I wrote that, I was busy running around. These days, I often sit in the evening and am happy to do nothing. Just sit."

"What about the dark end?" I asked.

"I don't think it's all dark. Something continues. It's as if the body and soul are tied together with little strings. The closer you get to leaving, the more the strings loosen and the more you connect with greater awareness, the expanded mind."

I said I've had intimations but no certainty of that happening.

"Look," he said. "There's a deep human fear of not being, not existing anymore. Either I survive bodily death in some way, or the whole machine is gonna turn off and that's the end—nothing. But if there's nothing, there'll be nobody around to be upset about it."

"That's what's frightening," I said. "Extinction. Much as I dislike parts of myself, the idea of being annihilated, no awareness of anything, ever . . ."

Reb Zalman raised his eyebrows and nodded. "I know how that feels in the gut. But I don't think it ends in oblivion. I'm curious—really curious to awaken to the larger picture." The glint came to his eyes. "Remember what Woody Allen said? 'I don't mind dying, I just don't want to be there when it happens.'"

Right.

"I *do* want to be there. I want to watch the last breath going out and whisper the Shema. I want to merge back with the infinite; I want to dissolve like a drop in the greater ocean."

I stopped typing for a moment. "That sounds kind of boring, just floating around in the ocean."

He started to laugh. "In the ocean I have a lot more than I have in my drop." He leaned forward. "Do you know what your past life was?"

Ah, yes. Better to get this out on the table. "I don't believe, literally, in past lives," I told him. "I can understand reincarnation as a metaphor or myth, but when someone tells me they remember being a queen or an army general, I start tuning out. No one seems to remember being a leper or a child molester."

Reb Zalman said there's a great deal of anecdotal evidence—people being hypnotized and remembering details from a past existence—that we've lived before.

"And there are a great many who dispute that evidence," I said.

"*Nu?* That's what makes for horse racing."

I asked if he's always felt at ease with dying.

"No. It came gradually. Liberal Judaism hasn't dealt

much with the afterlife, and since the Holocaust, hardly anyone speaks about it. The sense is that you live this life, and when you're dead, you're dead."

I remembered, as he said this, asking the warm and very modern Reform rabbi who confirmed me at age fifteen what happens when people die. He said, "There are several possibilities. Some people believe you live on in the good works you've done. Some believe in an ethical force that moves through all of us . . ." As he ticked off the other possibilities, I knew he believed none of them. My father, when I asked the same question, said, "We live on in the memories of others," an answer I found equally unsatisfactory.

Polls have consistently shown that Jews are far less likely to believe in an afterlife than people of other faiths. But Reb Zalman said there are Kabbalist texts with long passages about reincarnation and what's beyond this world, though they've never been translated into English. "The rationalists have held sway for the last hundred years, and they've wanted Judaism to be perceived as the religion of reason," he said. "So they buried the mystical. But the classical Jewish belief is that there are two worlds—this one and the world to come. At birth the soul enters the body, and at death the soul survives."

He urged me to go to the library and look in section 133 of the Dewey decimal system—the section on the occult and supernatural. "I read everything I could find there," he said. "In almost every culture, people have had visions of the afterlife, and they're remarkably similar. Also, the people who've had near-death experiences write that they felt so much light and love they were reluctant to come back. They felt so free."

I shook my head. "Near-death experiences don't prove that that's what actually happens when we die. I'm not saying it can't be true, but I prefer to hold it as a mystery."

Reb Zalman laughed. "That's fine. You leave a possible door open so there could be a surprise."

I told him about a book I'd read, *My Stroke of Insight*, by Jill Bolte Taylor, a brain scientist who suffered a massive near-fatal stroke that wiped out her ability to understand words. She remembers being in a state of bliss and oneness, however, not wanting to return to the speaking world.

Reb Zalman clapped his hands in excitement.

"But that could just be the brain," I said, "producing a chemical reaction that induces a sense of oneness and bliss."

Reb Zalman threw out his arms. "Isn't it wonderful that we should have such an illusion in those dire circumstances? We should thank Mother Nature for giving us that kind of illusion."

I couldn't resist laughing. He'd pulled the rug out from my mind's perpetual questioning.

"I don't want to convince you of anything," Reb Zalman said. "What I want is to loosen your mind."

What If It Ends in Nothing?

None of us seems psychologically able to cope
with the thought of our own state of death,
with the idea of a permanent unconsciousness
in which there is . . . simply nothing.
      —SHERWIN NULAND, M.D., *How We Die*

I can remember the moment I first understood—felt it in every cell of my being—that I would die. I was four, sitting at the kitchen table with my mother in our duplex apartment in Los Angeles. No one else was around. A friend of the family had died, and I asked her if everyone died.

Yes, she said.

"Are you going to die?"

"Yes, but not for a very long time."

"Am I going to die too?"

She nodded.

"What . . . what happens after you die?"

She didn't respond at first. I could see her considering what to say, watching my face, my whole four-year-old body contract with fear.

"You go to heaven," she said.

"Where is heaven?"

"It's a beautiful place, up above the world." She raised her arm and looked toward the ceiling. "Everyone you love will be there, and whatever you want—you just hold out your hand, say the word, and it will appear."

"Like . . . a banana split?" I said, naming my favorite dessert.

She nodded and held out her hand as if the banana with hot fudge and vanilla ice cream and slivered almonds and a cherry would drop into it.

I stared at her, wanting to believe this, willing myself with all my might to believe it. My mother had studied to be an actress, and she was giving it her best.

I saw her lips continue to move, but I didn't hear what she said. I had seen flowers die—turn brown, fall or blow away, and disintegrate into nothing. I stood and rushed to the bathroom, got down on my knees, and retched.

My reaction might have been less violent if my mother had truly believed in an afterlife. A friend who was raised Catholic said his mother told him he was going to heaven to be with Jesus and the angels, and he believed it and there was no problem. Until later, when he was a sophomore in college and suddenly knew he didn't believe it at all.

Since I had sensed, even at four, that my mother's depiction of heaven was impossible, I continued asking others. My father was said to be "good with death"—his last job before retiring was selling plots in a Jewish cemetery, which he called "the park." He told me that we all are like machines, and our gears wear down, get rusty, and eventually stop. He must have seen that this wasn't landing well, so he added, as if tossing me a flimsy rope, that we live on in the memories of the people we love. His mother, Sarah (I was named after her, but the "h" was dropped to make the name more "modern"), had died in her forties, before I was born, of a mysterious degenerative disease. Each time we went to temple, I watched my father stand and recite the Kaddish with tears in his eyes. Was that how she was living on, and if so, what would happen when my father and everyone else who'd known her died?

I recently heard Ira Glass on *This American Life* recount how as a child he'd been obsessed with death and equated it with sleep. "I knew I was going to die and my mom and dad couldn't help me. Nobody could help me. I'll be dead. Forever . . . Nobody would remember me or anybody that I had ever known. Forever." And the weirdest part, he said, was that "every night all the adults headed off for bed like this was no big deal. Complete annihilation. No big deal."

A more sensitive approach in discussing death with kids was taken by my friend Rachael Kessler, who died several years ago of cancer. At the memorial service, one of her grown sons described the conversation she'd had with him when he was young and a relative had died. He'd asked the same question I'd asked my mother, and Rachael had begun with the same response. Yes, you and I will die, but not for a long time. Then she said, "Does that make you sad?" He nodded. "It makes me sad too," she said. This had meant a great deal to the son—her honesty and authenticity—but I doubt it made the knowledge of mortality less frightening.

When I attended Sunday school at my Reform Jewish temple, I remember being irritated when my questions were answered with "These are things we cannot understand.

God has a greater plan that humans aren't capable of comprehending." In my twenties, however, as I began exploring other religious and mystical traditions, I was equally irritated when teachers gave elaborate descriptions and maps of what happens after death. The specifics of reincarnation or merging with some hazy notion of the infinite never rang true in me. My reasoning mind would pick the details to shreds. I came to see that this was my conundrum: I owned a seeker's heart and a skeptic's mind. The heart was like a pilgrim, walking with a staff, delighted when it encountered nuggets of wisdom, and the mind was quick to follow and point out flaws and contradictions.

What did ring true was the assertion at the root of most traditions that the answers are to be found within oneself. I learned to meditate, to do yoga and other spiritual practices, which brought feelings of calm and joy. Over the years, I experienced altered states of consciousness: of energy moving through me; of connecting with a force greater than the self; of oneness and, at times, boundless love and intimacy with everyone and everything, including "a tree, a rock, a cloud," as Carson McCullers wrote. The experiences would inevitably end but left imprints. I had felt the energy, felt the oneness as surely as I could feel the cold water when stepping into a mountain lake, and I stopped trying to explain such phenomena with the rational mind.

I took a workshop with Robert Thurman, the preeminent Tibetan Buddhist scholar (and father of the actress Uma Thurman), at a conference titled "The Art of Dying" in New York in 2000. Tibetan Buddhists believe that we pass through six *bardos*, or states of awareness, between dying and reincarnation. Thurman said that every day,

Tibetan monks practice traveling through the *bardos* so that when they die, the trip will be familiar. He led us in a guided meditation through the *bardos*, visualizing every state and ultimately merging with light. I found the process interesting and peaceful but couldn't help wondering what would happen to the Tibetans if the *bardos* prove not to be an accurate description of the afterlife.

Thurman said it's hard for Westerners to adopt the Tibetan model because we live in a material culture and the religion we believe in absolutely is science. We accept that black holes swallow up matter and earthquakes are caused by underground movements of tectonic plates, although most of us have had no direct experience of a black hole or a tectonic plate. When my son was four, an earthquake shook our home in California, sending books and dishes clattering to the floor. He came running to me in terror, and when I explained what it was, he looked puzzled. "I thought it was a giant walking up to our house."

In the workshop, Thurman said, "We believe life ends in nothing. Scratch a person who has faith in the afterlife and you'll find, buried under piles of concepts and hope, a fear that it all may lead to nothing. But there is no such thing as nothing!" he said. "There is no material 'nothing.' You can't isolate it, study it under a microscope, or enclose it in a black box. No scientist has ever succeeded in locating 'nothing.' So why do we have this core belief that life ends in nothing?"

Good question, I thought. And though the fear of nothing still seemed cemented in me, I allowed Thurman's words to play on the hard surface.

Shortly after moving to Boulder in 2002, I had an experience with a warm and articulate rabbi, Rami Shapiro, that caused further erosion of the cement. Rami, a younger colleague of Reb Zalman's, is also a poet and translator and so funny he could be a stand-up comic. I attended a daylong teaching he gave, in which we meditated, walked in silence, and had discussions, including one on the book of Job. At the end of the final meditation, Rami said, "I'd like you to keep your eyes closed and stay in that deep inner place. I'm going to ask a question, and just listen to what arises." We waited. Rami asked in a deep, rolling voice, "Where were you when I laid the foundations of the earth?"

I heard the word "present." That startled me. What could it mean? At the creation of the world I was . . . present? Deciding to press further, I asked: Is it possible I did not exist then?

I heard: no.

The words "Where were you when I laid the foundations of the earth?" are, of course, what God says to Job, who's led a devout and moral life, after Job implores God to explain why he's stripped him of everything—his house, his crops, all his possessions, his children, and finally his health. God unleashes a torrent of words, and when he's finished, Job is silent.

The traditional interpretation of Job's silence is that he's been humbled. It was God, not Job, who created the heavens and the world and all the wondrous and terrible things within and without, and Job accepts God's superior wisdom. But everyone at Rami's workshop—more than thirty people—heard the same message, unprompted, when asked, "Where were you . . . ?"

There.

Rami suggested that Job's silence is his awakening to the knowledge that he's part of it all—the whole carnival of creation, good and evil and everything in between—and he accepts it all. That resonated with me. Hearing the word "present" gave credence to intimations I've had that we are all connected in, for lack of a better word, Oneness, and that time may not be the straight line we take it to be.

So I came to my encounters with Reb Zalman feeling comfortable holding death as a mystery. Not knowing—the very state that had irritated me as a child in Sunday school.

I was also aware that most of the time we repress the knowledge of mortality, unless we have a close call—a car accident, after which we feel a heightened sense of the preciousness of life and gratitude for being here, still breathing. Writers like Carlos Castaneda urge us to remember that death is always an arm's length away. We hear that, know that, and then walk on, losing sight of the very thing that's an arm's length away.

Damien Hirst named one of his sculptures—a shark with mouth open and teeth gnashed together—"The Physical Impossibility of Death in the Mind of Someone Living." And Joan Didion, after writing *The Year of Magical Thinking* about losing her husband, John Dunne, told me, "I know I'm going to die, but not really. John's death made me look at it for John but not for myself. There's almost nothing that can make me accept that death will occur to me."

When I told this to Reb Zalman during one of our first meetings, he said, "I've been training myself since I was young for the moment I'll die." While riding the subway to the yeshiva in Brooklyn, he said, "I'd sit in the little compartment of the car originally intended for the conductor, only the conductor didn't sit there anymore." As a Hasid, Zalman was not permitted to see a woman's hair, hear her voice, or shake her hand unless she was a relative. "I didn't want to sit where all the other people sat and look at ads for Maidenform bras and get turned on," he said. "So I'd sit in the little compartment and imagine: I'm ready to go, I'm ready to go, and when I get to the Atlantic Avenue station I'll be gone. I'd say the Shema four or five times, thinking this is how I'll say it with my last breath."

He inhaled and let the air out slowly. He said he's also prepared his wife, Eve, who's twenty-four years younger, for that moment.

"How?" I asked.

"I told her, when it's my time, I'd like you to let me go."

"And her response was . . . ?"

Zalman smiled. "She said, 'Okay, on one condition: that you'll take me with you as far as you can.'"

I would make that deal.

3

Planning the Exit

Reb Zalman said he knows the hour he wants to die.

What hour? I asked.

"I'm not going to tell you."

I'd arrived for one of our first Friday meetings in a freak rainstorm that had caused parts of the basement to flood. Workmen were lifting the carpet and bringing in a machine to suction out water.

"Let's go into the chapel," Zalman said. "There's too much going on out here." I followed him into a small, dark, and windowless room, where three small orange lights are always burning, winking like Christmas tree ornaments.

"Isn't 'chapel' a Christian word?" I asked.

"So what?" he said. "People know what that means— it's my prayer room." But I've come to think of it as the rabbi's cave, because it feels like the caves I've visited in India and the Sinai desert, where monastics over the centuries have retreated to pray and meditate. Reb Zalman's cave is in the basement of a suburban home, but the air inside feels charged and enfolding. He's covered every inch of wall space with pictures of rabbis with beards and fur hats.

"That's the rogues' gallery," he said. He's also hung pictures of leaders of other faiths: Thomas Merton; Howard Thurman, an African-American mentor; a Sufi master; and a *thangka* of the Tibetan oracle, a gift from the Dalai Lama.

In the center of the room is a burgundy armchair where Reb Zalman prays; above it hangs a mobile of a Jewish star suspended inside a pyramid. Zalman looked up at it. "That's supposed to enhance what I'm doing."

Piled on his desk are books, charity boxes, and a roll-up piano so that "if a melody comes to me, I can record it." The charity boxes are destined for various organizations. "When I pray for somebody, I always take out a coin and put it in one of the boxes," he explained.

Reb Zalman was ordained in the Lubavitcher community, a Hasidic sect founded in the eighteenth century by the Baal Shem Tov—the Master of the Good Name. They're the men in long black coats and black fedoras you may have seen in cities around the country, driving a mitzvah-mobile, urging Jewish men to put on *tefillin*, small black prayer boxes with straps, and women to light Shabbat candles.

A portrait of the sixth leader of the group, Yosef Yitzchak Schneersohn, called the Lubavitcher Rebbe, hangs in the most prominent place in Reb Zalman's cave. Zalman had sought out the revered Rebbe soon after he and his family landed in New York, penniless, in 1941. The Rebbe received Zalman, then sixteen, in his study, and after listening to him describe his family's escape from the Nazis, arranged for his parents to work as furriers and for Zalman, his brothers, and sister to enter a yeshiva. Zalman walked out with tears flowing. "I felt that I had been fully seen—more than at any time in my life. And fully loved," he recalls. "I was ready to follow this guy to the ends of the earth."

As Reb Zalman settled into his prayer chair with his beloved rabbi behind him, I asked again at what hour he wants to die. He wagged a finger at me as if to say, "Nice try." "I'm not telling anyone, because if I die at a different time they'll be disappointed. But to me, the exit moment is important. I used to have a whole deathbed scenario planned. My wife would come and hold me, my Hasidim would be standing around, praying, and I'd have Albinoni's *Adagio for Organ and Strings* playing." He started humming it.

And now? I asked.

"I still want to be held, to feel a loving touch, but I don't need a whole big scene around me." He's also given up the elaborate plan he'd made for his funeral. "That's up to the people who're gonna remain. I don't need to boss anybody afterwards."

We laughed at that.

In the seventies, when he announced his plan for the disposal of his remains, it set off an uproar in the Hasidic community. He's decided against it now, but for years Reb Zalman wanted to be cremated, which violates Jewish law. I asked him why it's forbidden—something I'd never understood.

He said in the Rabbinic period, around 70 AD, wood was scarce in the holy land, and if bodies had been burned, the land would have been denuded of trees. Then he told a story from the Talmud asserting that cremation is an atrocity, a desecration of the body, which was formed in God's image. But the most common reason the Orthodox give for banning cremation, he said, is that "when the Messiah comes, God will resurrect all the bodies of the dead. The bones need to be preserved so they can be reconstituted."

Reb Zalman said he'd accepted that position until he visited Auschwitz in 1976. "I stood in front of the ovens where my uncle and cousins were burned and thought, 'Why was I spared? Why wasn't I among them?' I felt that kinship, you know?" He began to think that when he dies, "Why should I take up precious space in the earth? Wouldn't it make more sense, ecologically, to be returned to ashes? Then I could have mine sent to Auschwitz and joined with theirs." Zalman removed his glasses, cleaning them with the edge of his shirt. "I started speaking out, saying that cremation is the right thing to do, not a sin. I was quoted in a Jewish paper in Detroit, and you should see the trouble I had after that!"

Members of Chabad, as the Lubavitcher community is also known, called Reb Zalman and demanded that he recant what the newspaper quoted. Reb Zalman said, "No, that's what I said and what I meant."

Later he went to pray with a different Hasidic group in Brooklyn and heard two young men behind him discussing Zalman's heresy. "Why should we have to wait till he dies?" one said. "Let's burn him now."

An Orthodox man stopped Reb Zalman on the street, warning him that if he insists on cremation, "you won't be resurrected."

Reb Zalman nodded, thinking back to Vienna in 1938. His family was from rural Poland but was living in Vienna to work. As Hitler rose to power, Zalman's father had a strong knowing to flee with his family to the west. His brother, Akiva, who was also working in Vienna, wanted to return to Poland. "Akiva thought he'd be safe there because it wasn't under Hitler yet," Zalman recalled. "My father told him, 'No, we go west, we don't go to Poland. I'll share everything I have, every bite of food with you, but please, don't go back there.'" Akiva nevertheless returned to Oświęcim, Poland, where he was later arrested and forced to build concentration camps in the town, which the Germans renamed Auschwitz. Akiva and his family were among the first to be gassed.

Reb Zalman returned his attention to the man in black accosting him on the street in Brooklyn. "Okay," he said. "If God decides not to resurrect the people who were burned at Auschwitz, He can leave me out of it too."

4

Get Ready

Let me skip ahead to a conversation I remember as paradigmatic of how Reb Zalman intends to meet the dying of the light. I'm not going to proceed chronologically with this tale because our talks did not move forward in linear time. He would open a subject in January, reprise it in May, and a year later come back to it with a startling new slant, arising from ideas and events that had occurred in the interim.

The conversation I want to relate took place just before Passover. Eve, the rabbi's wife, who's also a singer, teacher, and therapist, was working in the kitchen with a volunteer. Wearing a long skirt, a loose blouse, and her silver, waist-length hair tied back with a ribbon, she projected a sense of joy and exhaustion. She'd spent the past week staying up till 3 A.M., going through all the closets, drawers, and shelves in the house. She was looking for *hametz*—anything with even a molecule of bread, flour, or wheat in it or any crumbs that might have lodged in a crevice. All *hametz* had to be removed from the house before the holiday.

I asked Eve, "Is this also like spring cleaning?" She looked up from wiping cupboards and gave a short laugh. "As long as I'm here, I might as well clean." Eve is credited by many, especially Zalman, with keeping him healthy.

The seders Reb Zalman conducts are legendary; they can last till 2 A.M. and are always different. He's led seders with ultraorthodox Hasidim, a seder with Catholic bishops and nuns where they recreated the Last Supper, and in the early 1970s, a seder where people took four puffs of marijuana instead of drinking four cups of wine.

When I went down to the basement and joined him in our chairs facing each other, he said a prayer asking blessings for our work. "What does Passover feel like in the December years?" I asked.

"That's such a good question. Give me a moment to go inside." He closed his eyes as he often does, waiting to sense what will arise. "When we come to the end of the seder, we open the door for Elijah the prophet. I ask everyone to be silent and think: What question would I like to ask the messenger of God?" He said people reflect on that, sitting quietly while the door is open, and after it's closed, he asks if they'd like to share what they heard from Elijah.

"Then we come to the place in the ceremony where Elijah asks, 'Are you ready to go?'"

"Go where?"

"Go forth from the seder into the world. But for me it's also, 'Are you ready to *go*?'"

He gave me the Look—a smile of mischief and enthusiasm I'd come to recognize as a signal that a story was on the way. "When I was a young rabbi in a small *shul* in Fall River, Massachusetts," he started, "they couldn't pay me enough to support my family, so I would also go to Providence,

Rhode Island, and work as a *shochet*—the kosher slaugh-terer." His name, Schachter, means "slaughterer," and for generations men in his family held that post, which was considered second in honor only to the rabbi.

He began to describe how he was trained to slaughter animals in a quick, merciful way and how the knife must be so sharp and smooth there are no bumps on it. I'd learned by this time that Zalman rarely answers a question directly. He tells a story, digresses to a different subject that reminds him of a memory, then sings a song until I have to strain to remember where the hell we started. I'm skilled at lassoing people back to the question I've posed, but Zalman can't be lassoed. No matter how much I tug, remind him, and cut in, he goes on in a circular pattern.

He proceeded to tell me how he worked in a shed behind the butcher shop in Providence. Most of the farmers, he said, brought in the chickens as if they were merchandise—they weren't living beings anymore. "I saw the chickens were thirsty, so I gave them water. Then I sent the chicken pluckers—a group of African-American men—out of the shed so I could speak to the birds. I told them, 'I'm not here to hurt you or be your enemy, but you have an opportunity to go from the level of animal to the level of human being by becoming food. I will help prepare you for that and try to do it in the most painless and sacred way.'"

I could picture him there in the slaughtering shed back in the 1950s, but how on earth would this tie back to the seder?

Reb Zalman said he called the pluckers back and started dispatching the chickens. "The pluckers were always talk-ing about their exploits the night before—the drinking, the women, and so on. I didn't like that conversation for what I needed to do. So as soon as they started plucking, I began singing spirituals, and they sang along with me."

He sang out, in his strong baritone, "Joshua fit the battle of Jericho, Jericho, Jericho," acting out how the pluckers would pull feathers in time to the beat. "They taught me a wonderful spiritual," he said, and started to sing "Travelin' Shoes."

> *Death come a knockin' at my mother's door,*
> *Hey, old woman, is you ready to go?*

Reb Zalman sang on, telling the story of how death comes knockin' at different people's doors—the mother, the father, the preacher—asking if they're ready to go. Each person says, "Yes, I done my duty, I been redeemed, I got on my travelin' shoes."

I wondered how many verses there were.

Then he sang that death comes knockin' at the sinner's door. The sinner says, "Oh, no, I ain't redeemed, I ain't ready, I ain't got on my travelin' shoes."

Reb Zalman smiled. "That's the song. That's what I'm aiming for."

"I'm not sure what you mean."

"When Elijah asks, 'Are you ready?' I want to be able to say: 'Yes, yes, I'm ready.'"

"Ready to go?"

He stood and began doing some soft-shoe dance moves. "I got on my travelin' shoes."

5

Where Could We Run?

There was a joke going around the Jewish quarter of Vienna in 1938: A man goes to a travel agent and asks, "Can you sell me a ticket to Uruguay or Paraguay?"

The agent says, "Do you have a baptismal certificate?"

"No, I'm Jewish," the man says.

"For a Jew, there's no place on this globe that I can sell you a ticket."

The man scratches his head. "Maybe you got another globe?"

Zalman was fourteen when Hitler annexed Austria in 1938. Overnight there were Nazi flags flying from the houses and people on the streets wearing armbands with swastikas. "We were shocked—how could it happen so fast?" Zalman recalled. "From that moment on, we were scared to walk on the street."

Zalman quit school to learn a trade so he could help feed his family, apprenticing himself to a weaver. One morning at the weaver's, he started having sharp pains in his lower right side. The only way home was on the trolley, but Zalman had to stand, bent over in agony, because only Aryans could take seats. When he finally arrived, his father bundled him into a cab and rushed him to the Rothschild Jewish Hospital, where a surgeon removed his appendix. Had it been an hour later, he was told, the appendix would have ruptured and he might have died of peritonitis.

Two nights later, lying on a cot in a ward with forty other men, Zalman heard crowds rampaging through the streets of Vienna, smashing the windows and looting stores owned by Jews—an event later known as *Kristallnacht*. Zalman's parents couldn't get out to visit him in the hospital. Toward midnight, a Gestapo squad of three men in black SS uniforms marched into the ward, looking for a man who'd been bayoneted and come to the hospital to have his wounds stitched up. The Nazis said he was a Bolshevik and accused the hospital of hiding an enemy of the Reich. They accosted the lone nurse on duty, asking for the man, and she pointed to a bed across the room from Zalman.

"Why did she betray that man?" I asked.

"When you see the SS guys, you pee your pants. You don't tell them to get lost."

The Gestapo approached the man, still unconscious from the anesthetic. "This man didn't need an operation; you wrapped him up as a disguise!" the Gestapo said, ripping off his bandages and cutting open his wounds. Zalman lay frozen in terror, knowing what was happening. The Gestapo marched out, and in a short time, the man bled to death.

When Zalman told me this story on a Friday in August—a perfect summer day with flowers blooming in voluptuous colors—his voice was calm and matter-of-fact. He described how in Vienna, after he'd been taken home to recover, he heard, at two in the morning, the boots of the police on the stairs to his family's door. They arrested his father, Shlomo, because his passport was invalid, but before Shlomo was dragged away, he took off his watch and gave it to Zalman. "You take my place now."

I told Zalman, "You were fourteen. Weren't you paralyzed with fear? Recalling it now doesn't seem to upset you."

Zalman closed his eyes and folded his arms across his stomach. "When I go back and ask, what's going on in my gut about this . . . ?" His voice grew animated. "It was like being in an adventure movie. I was frightened and I was excited. I know it's strange, but I didn't feel crushed by any of it. Papa was deported to Poland, but he snuck back on a train headed for Vienna." When they heard that the border to Holland would be open for twenty-four hours, the family made their way to the border. "I was still in pain from the appendectomy, but I was so excited I hardly noticed."

"This is hard for me to understand," I said. "I cry over much less. Weren't you anxious you'd be caught, tortured, and killed?"

Shaking his head, he said, "I felt all that when I visited Auschwitz forty years later. That's when it hit me—I was overcome with nausea and trembling. But at the time, we were making an escape and I was charged with adrenaline."

What about your father? I asked.

"His attitude was: never mind the guts and stuff. What do we have to do to survive? I think the same way."

When they reached the border to Holland, though, they were shut out. Despite their urgent pleas, they were told the border was closed—the rumor had been false. Officials gave them glasses of milk and escorted them onto a return train to Vienna.

Before the annexation in 1938, Zalman had been attending a secular high school in the morning and an Orthodox yeshiva in the afternoon, straddling two worlds. After Hitler took over, he said, there was no point learning Latin and algebra, let alone Hebrew. He began studying English on his own, hoping to get to England or North America. When the Gestapo stopped Jews on the street, they would ask, "Are you Aryan or are you learning English?"

But how could the family escape? The countries that bordered Austria to the west—Switzerland and Italy—were closed to Jews, and Shlomo felt strongly it wasn't safe to go east. Zalman told his father, "The Nazis will kill us all." Shlomo told him not to give up hope and arranged for them to take a train to Cologne, Germany. They had to pass through Germany to get to Belgium, the only country that might accept Jews who didn't have large sums of money. Shlomo had made contact with smugglers who'd agreed to guide them across the border between Germany and Belgium. But the smugglers didn't show up in Cologne. As hours passed, the family grew more terrified, but Shlomo found a man smuggling Leica cameras into Belgium who, after intense bargaining, agreed to take them across. When the family reached Antwerp, a policeman stopped them, demanding papers. "We cried," Zalman recalled. "We'd made it so far! We begged him, please don't send us back. The policeman softened—it was amazing to see—and he told us, 'You need some kind of identity. Go to city hall and they'll give you temporary papers.'" Zalman was given an identity card with the name, "the so-called Zalman Schachter," because he had no other papers to verify his name.

The following year in Belgium was to be a crucial one for Zalman, because it was there he first met Hasidim who were members of the Lubavitcher movement. Antwerp was a center for Jewish refugees, and many, like Zalman, found non-union jobs cutting diamonds or fur. While they worked, one would read from a Hasidic text, and sometimes they would stop to discuss it or they'd sing a *nigun*, a wordless melody intended to lift the soul. "These people were into a level of spirituality I hadn't seen anywhere else," Zalman recalls. He'd been brought up in a yeshiva where they memorized dry texts. At the *shul* he attended, the men davened, reciting prayers as fast as possible in a sing-song pattern, bending forward rhythmically at the waist in a motion that outsiders called "pecking." Zalman said, "Davening was something you rushed through. That's not what I saw from the people in Belgium. They showed me there was a deeper communion possible." The Lubavitchers believed that heartfelt prayer and song are as important as scholarly learning, Zalman explained.

The founder of Hasidism, called the Baal Shem Tov— the Master of the Good Name—had never gone to a yeshiva but had educated himself, coming to know God through devotion, singing, and prayer. Zalman said the Baal Shem told his followers that "the person who recites the psalms wholeheartedly is already on the same level or maybe even higher than the elite scholars."

When Zalman had arrived in Belgium, though, he was in no mood to sing God's praise. "I was angry with

God, and I thought everything I'd been taught at yeshiva was worthless. I wanted to fight." He made a fist. "And I couldn't fight Hitler or God, so I was looking for someone to stand in God's place." One afternoon, he knew that a group of young Orthodox men would be meeting with a teacher to study the *Ethics of the Fathers*, which begins, "All of Israel has a stake in the world to come." Zalman thought, "Oy, am I gonna give it to them." Standing by the door so he could run if things got ugly, Zalman announced that the world to come was "pie in the sky. Nobody has ever come back from there. It's baloney! Do you really believe that when the Messiah comes, the rivers are going to flow with wine, bagels will grow on trees, and the dead will crawl out from their graves to be resurrected? This is stupid! Opiate of the masses. Rob the people in this world but promise they'll get something in the next." Zalman said the students started shouting and wanted to attack him, but the teacher restrained them and said to Zalman, "Would you like to hear from someone who agrees with you?"

The teacher brought out a commentary by Maimonides, one of the most revered Jewish scholars, who lived in the Middle Ages, wrote *Guide for the Perplexed*, and was also a doctor and philosopher. Zalman recalled, "The teacher read a section where Maimonides debunks all the super-stitions about the afterlife." Paraphrasing Maimonides, Zalman said: "Just as a blind man doesn't know what color is, a deaf man doesn't know what music is, and a eunuch doesn't know what sex is, human beings can't comprehend the spiritual world. Most people who talk about the after-life don't know what they're talking about, because the afterlife is not felt with the body—it's felt with the soul. It's being with God, and there's a real presence; it's not merely an idea."

Hearing those words of Maimonides knocked the floor out from under Zalman. "It changed me. Maimonides was not only debunking foolish notions but affirming that there really is more than this physical world—there's a life of spirit. To hear someone as great as Maimonides say this made me feel I wasn't a fool or a heretic but someone who belongs," Zalman said. It was then, in Antwerp, that he began to make a deep commitment to Judaism. "And there were all these guys I could hang out with! I could sing with them, daven, meditate, and have conversations about higher things. I was home."

Then Hitler attacked Belgium.

6

Make Room for Intuition, and Listen

Reb Zalman was sneezing from a cold, his nose red and his eyes puffy. "I don't want you to catch it," he said when I walked down to the basement. Keeping a safe distance, he held out his arms in an embracing motion. "Consider yourself hugged."

He told me he'd woken up at three that morning and couldn't get back to sleep. He worked on the computer, and at five, he davened. "Then I had to go lie down again and reschedule my morning." He was troubled that he couldn't plan his days the way he used to. "I always felt that my body was carrying me. Now I'm carrying the body, telling it: 'Get up, walk, stop kvetching, you'll soon get to rest.'" He gave a rueful smile. "Adolescence, menopause—the changes that come about then are nothing compared to what happens to an elder."

The decline of the body seemed his toughest challenge. "The greatest depression comes when I expect my body to deliver what it did when I was younger." Recently he'd been sleeping with two oxygen tubes in his nostrils because of sleep apnea. He joked that he was becoming bionic. "I have lenses in my eyes, dentures in my mouth, hearing aids, a plastic patch in my diaphragm, and orthotics in my shoes."

He doesn't believe the physical deterioration can be reversed. "People tell me, 'Zalman, if you'd work out, swim so many laps, you could build up your body again.'" He raised his hands toward the ceiling. "My body said, 'Noooo, I don't want to do that. Don't flog the horse.'"

He assumed a pitiful expression that made me laugh.

"At the same time, I'm not giving up on the body. If someone tried to kill me with a knife, I would fight. I would not say, welcome—insert knife here." He was taking handfuls of vitamins and supplements and seeing a crew of healers, chiropractors, and body workers. "I've gone off coffee, off gluten, off this and that. I'm a good boy and I don't like it."

Are you sure all those steps are necessary?

"I don't know, but I'll do them anyway, for peace of mind. And for Eve and the kids."

He said he was beginning a critical part of the December Project—disidentifying with the body. If you were unable to move or use your body at all, the being you identify as You would still be present, he said. "Saint Francis spoke about the body as a donkey he was riding. He knew: I am *in* this body, but it's not what constitutes me."

"How do you maintain that dissociation when you can't sleep or a tumor is growing in your lung?" I asked.

He shook his head. "I'm not there yet. When I get cut, I say ouch. I haven't dissociated enough."

What would that be like? I wondered.

He leaned back in the rocker, shutting his eyes. "I'd be able to see myself sitting in the chair and feel compassion for the legs, for the stomach. I could say, 'Oy, poor body,' as if I were speaking to someone else. I'd feel free and un-encumbered."

What if there was severe pain?

"As I said, I'm not there yet. I'm talking about this be-cause I want people to see it's not all pleasant stuff in De-cember. The question is, what is the spirituality we need for this time?"

That's what I'd been asking him for weeks—what is the spiritual work of December?

He raised his hands as if surrendering to the sheriff. "Okay. Let me tell you. First, it's important to give yourself solitude—time to just sit and not do anything. Intuition is more important now than thinking, but you need to build a container for intuition."

How do you do that?

"There are contemplative tools, such as prayer, medi-tation, and reflection. The more you use those tools, the more attuned you'll become to intuition." He talked about Robert McNamara, who was secretary of defense during the Vietnam era. "When he was ninety, he could admit how wrong he'd been in escalating the war," Zalman said. "That was amazing—how did it happen? Because he had time to reflect."

I suggested that people could benefit from solitude and reflection at any age.

"That's true, but it's more pressing in December. It's part of the process of looking from a different vantage point, from behind the facade."

"What do you mean?"

He told me to put aside the computer. "I want you to have your hands free."

Reluctantly, I removed it from my lap but kept the voice recorder going.

"Imagine a line running from the front of your forehead to the back of your skull," he said. "Now imagine a line running horizontally between your two temples. Put yourself at the point where the two lines meet. Now look at your face, from the inside."

This was hard—trying to imagine what my eyeballs, nose, and set of teeth would look like from inside my head.

"See how you're constantly constructing a face, presenting yourself to the world—talking, smiling."

Okay.

"Now go down to your heart and breathe into that space in your chest."

This I could do.

"Start thinking from that place in your heart. For example, working on this book, we want to help people not freak out and be more at ease about dying. So this is an act of love."

I felt a relaxing in me, a softening, a letting down of the need to gather research efficiently. He asked me to return my attention to the face and open my eyes. When I did, Zalman's own face looked serene. Gone were the redness and puffiness brought on by the cold.

"You see, most of the time people never get out of their faces," he said. "Look at Michael Jackson—it was always his face, his face."

He continued, "If I go into my heart and invite God to spend some time with me there, that's a way of being cozy with God, rather than talking to . . ." He dropped his voice to a stentorian bass. ". . . the extragalactic super-duper one!"

I laughed. "At this moment, when you invite God, who or what are you inviting?"

"A source of cosmic compassion. Listen, any words I say are going to be wrong." In his book, *Jewish with Feeling*, he wrote, "GOD! Oy, what a word. What handful of letters in the history of the world has accumulated more baggage?" When he invites God into his heart, he said, "it's more that I'm creating a place—a place where we go when we want to recalibrate our truth and our goodness."

Warmth was easing through me, as on an early summer morning when the sun pours down like honey.

"For people in December to be able to say, 'Now I go into my heart. . . .'" He put his hand to his chest. "That's a beginning. Okay?"

He said that once people sense that they have a soul, a spark of the divine and the eternal within, "you can say to that spark, 'Teach me: What is true? Does the soul live on? Have I been incarnated before?' Then you wait. You don't push on to the next question. You leave time for truth to seep in, like a puddle slowly filling with water."

I told him I've tried this and the puddle hasn't filled.

He gave me a piercing look. "Keep listening."

7

Fleeing for Our Lives

"Hitler always started a new campaign on Friday. He had a superstition about that," Zalman said.

He was thinking back to the spring of 1940 in Belgium. His father, Shlomo, had just obtained special passports issued by the League of Nations for "stateless people," who had no citizenship in any country. On Thursday, May 9, Shlomo took their passports to the American embassy in Antwerp to apply for visas.

But on Friday, May 10, in the early morning darkness, Hitler unleashed his blitzkrieg attack on Belgium and the Netherlands. As if rising from hell, fighter bombers, tanks, and motorized artillery started converging on the cities. Small planes with machine guns were strafing the buildings, forcing people to take cover under their beds and tables.

At dawn on Monday, after hiding inside all weekend, Zalman's family rushed to the embassy to get their passports back but found long lines in front of the building and couldn't get in. "We heard the German tanks and artillery drawing closer," Zalman said. "We knew if we didn't get our passports by Tuesday, we'd have to run." When Tuesday passed with no results, they scrambled to the train station and climbed into open cars in a coal train headed for France. Pulling out, they heard shells hitting the station and saw flames shooting in the sky. All during the night they rode through explosions, smoke, and chaos, finally disembarking in Villebret, a town in southern France, where a farmer agreed to lodge them. Zalman, who was carrying a rucksack with the family's silver, sold a spoon to pay the farmer. But the French police soon appeared and hustled the family to a concentration camp for refugees from German countries. The French government had capitulated to Germany in 1939, signing an armistice agreement that required them to turn over to the Gestapo any refugees that Germany demanded.

I asked Zalman how his family was housed in the camp. He said the French had taken over a chateau once owned by a Jew. The soldiers were quartered in the chateau, and the Jewish refugees were put in the horse barns, where they slept on sacks filled with straw. Zalman's family of six had to live in one stall, "no larger than my prayer room," he said, pointing to the windowless alcove.

They were forced to work in the fields seven days a week. "I enjoyed cutting down trees and chopping firewood because we were accomplishing something," Zalman recalled. Then they were told to clear huge rocks from a stretch of land. "That was punishing—we had to wedge them and put a lot of force into uprooting them and dragging them across the field." They were hopeful, though, that after clearing the field their next task would be to plant potatoes and onions so they could supplement their rations.

As they were heaving the last boulder from the field, they were told the Gestapo would be coming the next morning to inspect the camp. Although the Nazis weren't occupying this part of France, the Vichy government set up after the armistice was cooperating with the Gestapo. The next morning, Zalman woke up to a sight that made him sink to his knees and vomit: three bodies hanging from ropes, their faces blue and swollen. The three had hung themselves because they didn't want to fall into Nazi hands.

When the Gestapo arrived, Zalman recalled, "the French soldiers looked like puny little boys next to the Germans in their great black coats and hats." The Jews were herded into a room, shaking with fear that some or all of them would be hauled away. "That didn't happen, thank God," Zalman said. Instead, the Gestapo demanded that the French smash and burn the latrines they'd built for the Jews—boards nailed together to make crude seats, with flies and insects swarming over them. The Gestapo instructed the French to build new ones and add lime to prevent contagion. "They told the French, 'If you want to kill Jews, do it, but you have to do it hygienically.'"

Shortly after the Gestapo had left, the French commander inspected the field the Jews had recently cleared and said, "Who gave you permission to remove those rocks? I want them put back." Zalman was crushed. "Any joy I'd had in the work was gone. He was giving us jobs just to demoralize us." Furious, he took a pickax, smacked it on a rock and it kicked back, knocking him to the ground unconscious. His father tried to run to him but was restrained by the guards. Forced to keep working, Shlomo had to watch from a distance as Zalman lay motionless. Was he breathing? At length a dog came and licked Zalman's face, and he woke up, dragging himself back to work. "I had terrible migraines after that," he said.

When Paris fell to the Nazis one month later, the police let Zalman's family go. "We were below the Vichy line in unoccupied France, which saved our skins," he said. The family made its way to Marseilles, where they hoped to book passage to America. They found lodging with other Jews in a poor, overcrowded neighborhood while they waited through many delays for their visas to be processed.

Zalman, then sixteen, found several young Lubavitchers and met an older rabbi whom he asked, "Could you find somebody to teach us Torah? There's nowhere here we can learn." The rabbi arranged for a yeshiva graduate from Antwerp to hold classes with Zalman's group. "We organized a sort of yeshiva to sit and study . . ."

"Wait," I interrupted him. "How could you sit and study Torah when the Jewish community was being obliterated? You'd been thrown into a camp where you had to heave boulders back and forth and were sleeping six to one horse stall . . ."

"And I was in love with Fernande Gutking," Zalman said. "She was a girl my age I had met at the camp. Every day I would write her love letters in Flemish. And I liked to go walking through the streets of Marseilles. I was curious about the starfish that were unloaded at the dock. I found out the fishmonger was throwing away the heads of most fish, so I gave him twenty francs for a whole bag of heads. We cooked them, and enough flesh fell off the bones that we had some protein to eat."

"What happened to Fernande?" I asked.

He let out a sigh. "I'm very much afraid she was caught. I used to have a fantasy when I was in Brooklyn at the yeshiva, that the bus would stop and Fernande would come off the bus."

I was startled that Zalman could be a curious tourist, fall in love with a fellow refugee, and study texts praising God while Jews were being exterminated. What happened to your anger at God? I asked. He closed his eyes, moving his head from side to side. "You have to understand the root of the anger. The root was that the God that had been given to me, the God that would always protect Israel—that God had finked out. Did my anger mean that I didn't want God anymore? No. But that idea of God had to be shattered, and when it was, a different idea of God, a more universal God of spirit could take its place. So the same energy I'd thrown into anger I could now throw into pursuit of that spirit."

Besides, he said, "I don't go by the rearview mirror. Some people always look backward, but my notion is: What do we do next?" He told me to consider the good things that happened. "Coming to Belgium, I was introduced to the Lubavitchers. Coming to the camp, I found such a sweet love with Fernande. Coming to Marseilles, I met the man who would become the seventh Lubavitcher Rebbe and my mentor, although I had no idea who he was at the time."

That man, Rabbi Menachem Mendel Schneerson, came once as a guest speaker when the regular teacher couldn't be present. Menachem was in his thirties and looked nothing like the other Hasidic teachers Zalman had known, with straggly beards, long black coats, and black hats. "This man wore a gray business suit and gray fedora, and his beard was neatly tucked under his chin," Zalman said. "He carried himself with great dignity."

Menachem gave what Zalman thought was a brilliant teaching, drawing on his knowledge of not only Hasidism but secular history and science. "I found out he'd studied engineering and math at the Sorbonne, and I thought, this guy could show me how to reconcile religion and science." Zalman also felt the teacher's vulnerability and compassion. Menachem had close relatives who couldn't get out of Poland, and when he discussed the suffering in Jewish communities, he would cough into his fist to cover his tears.

After Menachem had left, Zalman learned that this man in the gray business suit was the son-in-law of the sixth Lubavitcher Rebbe, who'd been rescued from Poland and transported to Brooklyn, where he was leading the worldwide Lubavitcher movement. Zalman vowed that when he reached the United States, he would seek out the Lubavitcher Rebbe.

Using their last resources, the family bought steerage tickets on a boat that sailed from Marseilles to Spain, Algeria, Morocco, Senegal, and then to the Virgin Islands, where, after clearing customs, they walked out into the warm Caribbean air and were—could it be?—free people! "The relief we felt—it can't be described," he said. "The whole time I was on the French ship, under the French umbrella, I didn't feel safe. But once the U.S. authorities stamped our papers, we had escaped! I didn't kiss the ground because I was gaga looking around." After the monotony of being on the boat, staring at water, he saw banana trees, enormous birds of paradise, pink and blue pastel buildings, and everyone speaking English.

The Schachters caught another boat to Puerto Rico and a third to New York, by which time they'd been at sea almost three months. "We survived on canned sardines. That's all we ate—bread and sardines—along with lemons Papa secured so we wouldn't get scurvy." Zalman smiled. "I still have a fondness for sardines."

What? Most people wouldn't want to touch a sardine after subsisting on them for months, forcing the oily gray things down every day so their bodies could have fuel, but Zalman, I was learning, is wired differently. "You keep asking me," he said, "why talking about this doesn't stir up bad feelings. Of course I felt pain—I was angry and bitter going through it. I had a friend in school in Vienna, Hans, who wasn't Jewish. He was poor, and every day I would share my lunches with him. Later he became a Hitler youth, and while his clothes used to be ragged, now he was wearing a crisp black uniform."

Zalman shook his head from side to side. "He made me stand in front of a Jewish store wearing a sign that said, 'Aryans, don't buy from a Jew!' and do deep knee bends. He knew I'd just had my appendix out, and doing knee bends felt like my guts were being ripped apart." The next week, Hans and two cronies forced Zalman and another Jewish boy down to the Danube and beat them. "They started to cut off the *payos* [sidelocks] from my friend, and I could have kicked them into the Danube, I was in such a rage. But I didn't dare, because an SS man by the river was playing with his Luger, watching the whole business. If we'd hurt those boys, our families would have been punished." They had to let themselves get socked and kicked until they could barely crawl home.

Zalman raised his eyebrows. "The question is, how deep did all those feelings take root? Do I still have them seeded in me someplace?" He closed his eyes, as if to search every corner and crevice. "No."

"Was it an effort to let go of those feelings, or did it just happen over time?"

"I'll tell you a strange story," he said. "When King David had his liaison with Bathsheba, they had a baby. The baby grew sick and looked like it was going to die. David put sack cloth and ashes on himself, crying and praying. He prayed and prayed, but the baby died. Then he got up, bathed and dressed himself, and went off to compose a psalm. So the question people asked was, 'How come you're not mourning?' David said: 'As long as the baby was alive, I had hope that he could recover, so I prayed. Now that the baby is dead, there's nothing I can do.'"

Zalman stared at me, making sure I was taking this in.

"That feels so cold-blooded," he said, "but I have a certain sympathy for it."

"So do I. I just don't embody it."

He laughed, shrugging his shoulders as if to say, *Nu?*

"I would like to," I said.

"Hang around."

8

Dealing with Pain and Memory Loss

I found Reb Zalman coughing and short of breath the next Friday. He'd been carrying one of his cats up the stairs from his basement when the cat started squirming and clawing. "So I started going up faster, and when I reached the top, I was gasping so much I felt, if I had to climb one more stair, I would have a heart attack."

He said he's been thinking hard about what he needs "to meet the steep decline of the body." When he lies down and imagines, "Okay, this will be my last breath," there's no problem, he said. "I have all kinds of serenity about dying, but I do not feel serene when I can't get enough air or my inner organs don't feel aligned and I can't move freely. I start to worry, am I gonna get cystic fibrosis?"

"Why would you think that?"

"Something in the lungs is not right."

Coughing again, he moved his chair three feet away from mine. Usually we sat knee to knee, so the recorders could capture both our voices.

Zalman picked up the question: "What kind of awareness do I need so I don't get freaked out? When I'm struggling for breath and adrenaline is rushing through me saying, 'Warning, red alert!' how do I manage that? I need a kind of spiritual armament that I don't quite have yet."

What might that be?

He reflected a moment. "Learning to meditate between the contractions. Picture a woman giving birth. When the contractions and pain come, you can't do anything but ride them. But in between the contractions, you can meditate, pray, attune to the soul. In between, I can do that. But when it's happening . . ."

"I guess you just have to surrender more . . ."

"Yah! That's easy for you to say."

"That's *my* line," I told him.

He laughed, as if to say, your point, and pulled a crocheted afghan over his legs. When he's home, Reb Zalman dresses for comfort, wearing sweatpants, cozy sweaters, and socks that don't necessarily match, but there's always a yarmulke on his head.

I told him I worry more about the decline of the mind than the body. Most people, I've found, are more frightened of losing what they consider their mind—the ability to think, remember, and speak—than of physical illness, because it seems like it would be losing one's core intelligence, becoming an imbecile.

During the past year, my sister, Terry, and I had made the hard decision to move our ninety-five-year-old mother, Alice, to a care home for people with Alzheimer's. Alice had always been strong willed and demanding, a fiery real estate agent who was a life master in bridge and a maven of musical theater. She'd told Terry and me never to put her in a care facility, but in her eighties, she began to forget the conversation she'd just had or the movie she'd just watched. When I drove her to San Diego to visit my son in college, he asked her, "Grandma, do you know where you are?"

"Yes," she said, looking around. "I'm in Italy."

By the time she turned ninety, she needed a caregiver to make sure she didn't leave a pot on the stove and burn down her condo. She knew who we were and insisted she could still drive, but Terry and I were afraid she might hurt herself and others. I told the caregiver to remove the car keys from Alice's purse, but when she found out, Alice called me in a rage. "How dare you make decisions for me! I'm over twenty-one. You have no right to stop me from driving!"

"Mom, we're concerned about your safety . . ."

She slammed down the phone, and I stood for five minutes, taking deep breaths. Then I called her back.

"Sara," she said. "How nice to hear from you."

She'd forgotten she was angry at me.

What surprised me most was that she wasn't troubled by her inability to remember anything outside the moment. Terry had heard about a new drug being tested on Alzheimer's patients that was reputed to restore their memory. When we asked Alice if she wanted to participate in the trial, she shook her head.

"Mom," I said, "if you could take a pill that would let you remember everything, would you want to do that?"

"No. I'm fine the way I am," she said. "What do you want me to remember?"

"Well, your granddaughter just got married, and you walked down the aisle and danced. Wouldn't you like to remember those happy occasions?" She thought a moment.

"There are a lot of unpleasant things too." She knocked wood—the table. "I'm fine the way I am."

It was painful to watch her mind fading—it seemed an awful finale, and it could be me in twenty years. Both of Alice's parents had suffered dementia, and I'd read that there's a genetic predisposition. I told Reb Zalman, "I can feel my memory slipping—yours is in better shape than mine, and you're two decades older. I want to be at ease with what's going to happen but . . . how do I face this with equanimity?"

Zalman said there's a bright side: people with dementia are living completely in the present. I'd noted that. When Alice began showing signs of senility, she underwent a radical personality change. She became what I later learned was called "pleasantly demented." While I was growing up, we used to call her the "send-back queen," because she rarely had a meal in a restaurant where she didn't send food back. But now she was happy all the time, pleased to eat anything dropped on her plate. She did not complain when she was moved to the care home, and even after she'd taken a severe fall there, when I asked how she was, she replied, "Wonderful." Why couldn't she have been this way when we were growing up?

I told Zalman she seems to have attained qualities we associate with enlightenment: accepting what is, being fully in the moment, not criticizing or judging because she has no memory to compare anything with. "She's not functional, she doesn't know what day it is or where her clothes are, but she has the equanimity that Buddhists and yogis are aiming for."

Zalman smiled, saying he'd heard of cases like hers.

I told him what Oliver Sacks, the celebrated neurologist and author, had said when I interviewed him for an article in *Newsweek* about pleasant dementia. Sacks was familiar with the state and said it had come to Ralph Waldo Emerson in his seventies, when he developed what today would be diagnosed as Alzheimer's. At lectures he would read his notes aloud, joking later that he was "a lecturer who has no idea what he's lecturing about." Yet he told friends he was "quite well. I have lost my mental faculties but am perfectly well."

Not me, I told Zalman. I panic every time I have a memory lapse. Just the previous week, I'd received an e-mail from a woman saying she was coming to Denver and asking, "Could I stay in your house?" The name was not familiar, and I searched my brain: Who the hell was she? I even found her picture on Google and didn't recognize the face. Either she knew me well enough to invite herself to stay with me, or she had outrageous chutzpah. I sent her an e-mail I thought was tactful: "I'm having some memory issues these days. I have the sense that I saw you not long ago, but can't remember where or when. Could you remind me—when did we last see each other?"

A few hours after pushing "send," it came to me. Good God, she was a woman I'd met in Aspen and stayed with for a week when I was taking a ski course. I'd eaten with her family and we'd exchanged e-mails afterward. And that was only three months ago.

Zalman leaned his head toward me. "This is what gives you worry?"

It does.

Closing his eyes, he said that when he asks, "Who is Zalman, what is he made of?" he starts by looking at his body, his mind, his feelings, then goes deeper until, he said, he arrives at an interior space where the outside is not so interesting. "If we cultivate the interior—where the One who makes it all happen is present—we don't need the outer memories."

Really?

"All the details—who is that woman and when did we meet—are not so important. What's more important is: Do I sense the field around me? Do I appreciate the specialness of the moment? Do I feel consciousness, awareness, presence—it goes by many names. All these wonderful things . . . they don't happen on the outside."

What he was saying began to land.

"I believe that if you find more time to spend in that inner space, it will help you," Zalman said.

I would agree. But I can't help asking, "If you lose your memory, what happens to consciousness? Are you still aware of 'the One who makes it all happen'? I'm afraid of losing that as well. Becoming a zombie, a body ticking on after consciousness has departed."

Zalman shook his head vigorously. "When I have a memory lapse, I don't lose the sense that I exist, that I am." He described, with some pain, how he was once dancing with a woman at a holiday party, even kissed her cheek, and suddenly couldn't remember who she was. He couldn't recall not just her name but any detail about her or how he knew her—right in the middle of the dance. "I had the feeling, I'm still present, I'm aware, and I'm struggling to figure out who this person is. It took about five minutes before it came back. But in the middle of the lapse, my I-am-ness was there. It's not like I was in a coma."

He said people with dementia often repeat the same question, no matter how many times you answer it. "They're trying to get hold of exterior reality. But there's still an inner consciousness, a presence that can feel and receive."

I'd observed this with my mother; when I speak to her and tell her I love her, she responds.

"So, when you have a memory lapse," Zalman said, "think about meditating between the contractions. Go to your heart and connect with 'I am.'"

I felt relief. "I've been trying to talk myself out of being scared of developing Alzheimer's, because pleasant dementia looks like an easier way out than being wracked with pain from cancer. But that hasn't worked. Each time I forget something, I'm frantic. Is this the beginning of the end?"

Zalman looked surprised. "Well, it *is* the beginning of the end." He laughed. "But you've still got a long way to go." He started to sing "It's a Long Way to Tipperary," pumping his arm to the beat. It's a rare session with Reb Zalman, I thought, when he doesn't break into song.

I couldn't resist singing with him; the mood in the basement had become about a hundred times lighter.

"Thank you."

"You're so welcome," Zalman said. "Oy, are you welcome."

9

A Soldier in the Rebbe's Army

When Zalman was seventeen, a yeshiva student in Brooklyn, he wore a sleeveless undershirt with ritual fringes, or *tzitzit*, attached, a shirt and jacket over that, and a beret over his yarmulke. On a winter morning in 1943, he walked with slow, mindful steps toward the office of his Rebbe, his master, the leader of Chabad, the sixth Lubavitcher Rebbe—Yosef Yitzchak Schneersohn. (I'll refer to him as "the Rebbe" or "r-YY".) It had been two years since Zalman entered the yeshiva, after his first meeting with the Rebbe on arriving in New York.

At the door to the Rebbe's study, Zalman kissed the mezuzah and silently approached the desk. Following custom, he placed a question he'd written before the Rebbe. He felt he wasn't going deep enough in his prayers and wanted to know why. He stepped back and sucked in his breath. The Rebbe sighed and averted his eyes, tuning in not only to Zalman at that moment, his followers believed, but to the entire sweep of Zalman's life—past and future.

Zalman waited, fearing what the Rebbe might say. At length, the Rebbe turned his eyes to Zalman with heartfelt goodwill. "Every country has its proverbs," he said. "In America, it's 'Take it easy.' If you want to go deep . . . just take it easy." Then the white-haired Rebbe who could barely walk put his hands on Zalman to give him a blessing.

It wasn't the words, Zalman told me decades later, but the love transmitted to him that bonded Zalman to the Rebbe. "I could talk to him about my inner life, and he would give me directions. He made me a Hasid. When he'd sing or pray, I could attune to his heart." Zalman felt that no other group could match what the Lubavitchers were doing with the Rebbe. Other Orthodox sects were fussing about externals, debating which cuts of meats were the most kosher, but the Lubavitchers focused on the experience of prayer, meditation, and song, on drawing close to God.

Zalman said everything he teaches today is rooted in Chabad.

"That's strange," I said, "because Chabad seems the opposite of Jewish Renewal. The Lubavitcher men look archaic and unapproachable, wearing black coats from the Middle Ages and refusing to shake a woman's hand. They're like the Amish driving buggies."

Zalman laughed. "They're regular army. I'm CIA."

"What? The CIA spies and kills . . ."

"But they don't follow the usual rules," Zalman said. "Jewish Renewal doesn't follow all the rules. We update some of them."

At the yeshiva, however, Zalman took pride in being regular army. He was given a little room at 770 Eastern Parkway, a three-story red brick building that contained the living quarters and study rooms of the Rebbe.

If he woke up early enough, before dawn, Zalman would

take the trolley to the *mikvah*, the ritual bathhouse, in East New York. Undressing, he would submerge himself four times in the water, reciting a different prayer with a different intention each time. He had to be back at the yeshiva by seven-thirty, when the first class began. At nine they did the morning prayer and at ten ate breakfast, then prepared for the day's lecture on Talmud.

Lunch was at one in the basement of 770. Zalman said they had a female cook "who made wonderful meatballs and potatoes, but you weren't supposed to enjoy it too much. You ate to sustain your body so you could study and pray, so the rule was: don't be a glutton and eat for pleasure." He paused, then cracked a smile. "But on Shabbos, you may!"

The boys alternately studied and prayed in the yeshiva until nine at night.

"How did you find that regimen?" I asked.

"Ohhhhh, it was heaven!"

"Because when I hear the details . . . it sounds awful."

"I tell you, it felt like a shoe that fits. I was so hungry for that learning!" He believed the world was created so people could learn Torah and serve God.

I asked what his relationship to God felt like at the time.

"You can't imagine how much in love with God I was." In the morning, he recalled, when he put on his shoes, "I put on the right shoe first, then the left, and tied the left shoe first, then the right, because that's the way it's suggested in the code of Jewish law. And all the time, I was winking up at God. 'See? I'm doing it the way you want me to.'"

And was God listening and responding?

"Yes, yes." Zalman looked wistful. "Sometimes I long

for the longing I had for God then. It was bliss, like a lover with his beloved."

He was also in thrall with his Rebbe, and liked to hear stories about his life. R-YY had been born in Lubavitch, Russia, and when the Soviets came to power, he was determined to preserve Jewish spiritual life. He was arrested and beaten, but he always said that under no threat would he give up his religious activities. One Soviet agent held a gun to the Rebbe's temple and said, "This little toy has made many a man change his mind." The Rebbe answered, "That can only intimidate a man who has many gods and one world to serve them in. Because I have only one God and many worlds in which I can serve, I am not impressed by your little toy."

The Rebbe was forced to leave Russia and eventually made his way to Warsaw, where he tried to help Polish Jews evade the Nazis. He would have been sent to Auschwitz himself if U.S. senators and world leaders hadn't pressured Germany to grant him immunity. Weakened and in poor health, the Rebbe arrived in New York by boat in 1940, announcing that he had come not for his own safety but for a mission: to rebuild Orthodox Judaism in a free land.

By the time he died, in 1950, Chabad was a dynamic community, where at all hours you could hear passionate prayer, music, and dancing. The challenge was: r-YY had left no son to succeed him.

He did, however, have a son-in-law, Menachem Mendel Schneerson (whom I will call r-MM). This was the man in the gray business suit who had spoken at Zalman's little makeshift yeshiva in Marseilles and so impressed Zalman with his mastery of science and religion that Zalman resolved to seek out the Lubavitchers in New York. R-MM later settled in Brooklyn himself, and a year after his father-in-law died, he was affirmed the seventh Lubavitcher Rebbe.

Over the next four decades, r-MM greatly expanded Chabad's influence in the world, and he was revered for his brilliance and judgment not only by Hasidim but people from other faiths.

Zalman transferred his allegiance from r-YY to r-MM, but the relationship was different. He'd been a teenager needing love and guidance from r-YY, but he was twenty-six, ordained and launched as a rabbi, when r-MM took the seat.

Four years earlier, in 1947, Zalman had gone before three heads of the yeshiva, who grilled him to determine, as Zalman put it later, "what you knew and if the area of your not-knowing was respectable." Zalman's stomach was knotted with anxiety, but at the end of the exam, his inter-rogators said, "Mazel tov!" and shook his hand. The next morning he received a certificate of ordination.

Zalman was joyful when r-MM became the Rebbe. "I felt he was doing great stuff, conquering America and the world. But I couldn't attune to his heart the way I'd done with his predecessor."

Zalman explained that the relationship between rebbe and Hasid is like that of guru and devotee. "You give power of attorney over your life to your rebbe. You become an appendage of his, but I didn't want to be an appendage. I wanted to learn how to be a master myself."

To that end, Zalman stayed in close contact with r-MM, returning to his *shul* to pray and listen to his teachings. He sent him copies of letters of spiritual guidance that Zalman wrote to his own students, and r-MM would make suggestions in the margins. "It was like an apprenticeship," he said.

This continued while Zalman served as rabbi at small *shuls* in Fall River and New Bedford, Massachusetts, and when he moved to Winnipeg, Canada, to teach Jewish studies at the University of Manitoba.

But Zalman was restless. He asked the Rebbe if he could go to Bombay, India, to be rabbi of a congregation that was in decline and needed a leader. "I wanted to preserve their ethnic traditions and stories before they were lost." The Rebbe said no. Later Zalman sent the Rebbe a proposal to start a satellite Lubavitcher center on Wall Street, like a Christian Science reading room. "What was going on in Brooklyn needed to be brought to the financial district, so people could come in and say Kaddish, daven, and have a cup of tea." The Rebbe said no.

Zalman was angry. "Why was the Rebbe keeping me in Winnipeg when I could do greater things in the world?" On his next trip to Brooklyn, Zalman walked into the community room fuming, rehearsing what he'd say. But when the Rebbe entered for the evening prayer, he was coughing badly and looked exhausted. Zalman realized that the Rebbe had never taken a day off. He worked all hours, making himself available to everyone who had a need. Zalman's anger melted. Never mind, he told himself, I'm not gonna rebel.

When Zalman met with the Rebbe, he began, "Since you've said no to this and no to that, here's my feeling: You program me. You call the shots, and I'll jump where you tell me to go."

The Rebbe looked at him a long time and shook his head. "What you're describing is death," he said. "If you give over your will, you become a robot. God doesn't want that."

Repeating this to me decades later, Zalman said, "I thought that was remarkable . . ."

"Wait," I said. "Did that mean you were free to go where you wanted?"

"No. I stayed in Winnipeg." The familiar glint of play-fulness came to his eyes. "But I didn't keep the blinders on."

The Rebbe was not the only person who didn't always sup-port Zalman's expanding interests. His wife had been raised and groomed for her role in the Lubavitcher community. Their marriage had been arranged in 1945, when he was nineteen and she was twenty-two. As a yeshiva student, Zalman had never been on a date or even spoken at length with a female outside his family. He wasn't permitted to read books or watch movies about romance and relation-ships. When he was introduced to the woman who'd been selected by the *shadchan*, the matchmaker, they couldn't go to a regular movie so they went to see a newsreel. Zalman told me that hanging out with a girl in any way, even watching a newsreel, was a new and potent experience. He didn't ask himself if he loved her. "I was a card-carrying Lubavitcher and wanted to marry another card-carrying member of the Rebbe's army. The only question was, could she fulfill the duties of a Hasidic wife: to have children, cook kosher meals, and keep Shabbos?" His way of pro-posing was to say, "Should we ask the Rebbe already if we should get married?"

When he went to see the Rebbe for a blessing before his

marriage, the Rebbe said, "You have to understand what a woman is all about." Zalman nodded, but he did not understand. "I had no idea what a woman thinks like, but I didn't have the chutzpah to say, '*Nu*, could you please explain that to me?' I had no knowledge of anatomy or how sexual organs work. And neither did she."

The community didn't offer any teaching or instruction? I wondered.

Zalman shook his head. "What they teach you is how to watch the girl to see when she has her period. You have to wait so many days until she can bathe in the *mikvah* and become purified again before you can get it on."

She was an ideal wife for a yeshiva student committed to becoming a rabbi. They were together for twenty-two years and raised five children. But when Zalman began to delve into ideas outside Hasidism, she wanted to hold to the precepts she'd been taught. "I don't want to fault her," Zalman told me. "She stretched as far as she could, and I stretched as far as I could." A sweetness came to his voice as he spoke about her, and his eyes looked wistful. "We really did try to love each other."

10

Can We Choose When to Die?

I came upon Reb Zalman lying barefoot on his back on the carpet of the basement, his feet strapped to a machine that was shaking them, making his legs, hips, and torso vibrate. "It's good for the circulation," he said. His legs had been swelling, so he'd bought the machine from a local healer. He explained that it's like doing qigong exercises, only the machine does it for you. "Try it."

I got down on the floor, and he strapped my feet in. With a whir, the machine jumped to life, making my whole lower body chatter and rattle. "Okay, I get the idea."

As I set up my computer, I realized that I'd left my digital voice recorder at home. Should I go back for it? No, Zalman said, beckoning me into his computer room, where every surface was covered with jumbles of papers, wires, machines, and techno clutter. He picked up a large glass fishbowl filled with a dozen voice recorders! It was like a collection of matchbooks. How could he need that many? He said I should borrow one, and I reached in as if it were a grab bag.

We were about to discuss a blog I was writing about

Reb Zalman for the *New York Times* online, on caring for parents who seem close to dying. We began, as we often did, with a prayer. "Dear God," Zalman said, "as people grow older they need to have a sense of your presence in their lives. So please, give us the right words and the right intention. We ask that whatever our two souls have to do together here . . ."

He thought a moment, then shrugged. "It shouldn't not happen."

"Amen," I said with a laugh.

I told him that my ninety-five-year-old mother, who had Alzheimer's but still recognized us, never spoke about dying or God. I wondered if she was in denial or at peace, and what I could do to help her make the transition with grace and love. "I can't just blurt out, 'Mom, you're dying. How does it feel?'"

"No. You don't have to tell her that," Zalman said. "Just sit with her quietly and think about what you love and appreciate in her. She's going to a different place, and you'll be missing her. Your thoughts and feelings will get through."

Others had asked him the same question. A poet in San Francisco said her parents had never been religious. "I can't talk to them about *bardos* or the world to come . . ."

Zalman shook his head. "Their generation had a different task than yours. Look at what they had to go through—growing up during the Depression. They were worried about surviving, providing a house and food so their families would be secure. They had to focus on material things. You don't go to them now and say, 'What do you think will happen to your soul when you drop your body?' They'll look at you like you're *meshugge*."

He wanted younger people to remember, "It's their death. This is not about you. Let them have their choice, even to the last minute."

What he said next startled me. "If parents say they're ready to go, let them make that decision."

Are you suggesting we allow them to commit suicide?

"Not by taking pills or putting a gun to their head. But they can stop eating and drinking."

How is that not suicide?

He said there's a "big distinction between active suicide—taking pills—and passive suicide, which is just a decision: I don't want to eat anymore." If you take pills, he added, you may regret it but it's too late. Whereas if you stop eating, on the third or fourth day, you could change your mind and say, "All right, I want to stick around, let me have some food."

"Whether it's active or passive, you're still taking your life, and Jewish law says that's forbidden. How can you say it's permissible?"

Zalman said he feels there's a gray area between what's forbidden and permitted. "If I eat pork on Yom Kippur, that's a super no-no. Eating kosher chicken on Shabbos is a super yes-yes. But imagine I'm going to the Olive Garden and having a salad. The plates are not kosher, but the ingredients in the salad are not *traif* (unclean). You could choose to eat the salad."

He said that if a man shoots himself, it's like eating pork on Yom Kippur. And enduring terrible pain to the last breath is like eating kosher chicken. "But in between there are options—that's the gray area."

"It's slippery ground. Why do you want to go into this?"

"I know if I state that suicide is okay, I'm in trouble," Zalman said. He doesn't believe young people should be able to take their lives because they've been dumped by a lover or failed a test. "That's a super-duper no-no. But we're talking about people in the December years, who see the horizon of their life closing in on them. If they dread losing control of their bodies, if they're afraid of excruciating pain that has no cure, they may want to know that when they're ready, they can cut out."

A man in Zalman's community who was suffering from ALS, Lou Gehrig's disease, had asked Zalman if he could take an overdose of pills before the disease spread to his lungs and brain. Zalman said that wasn't necessary; he could choose to stop eating. "Knowing he had that choice gave him control. He wasn't at the mercy of intolerable pain." And because he had that freedom, Zalman added, he was able to stay around longer than he'd imagined.

Would you make that choice? I asked.

He said he can't know. "If there's tremendous pain, will I say, I'm going to stop eating and make my way out? Or will I say, Okay, as long as it pleases you, God, that I should experience this, I will do that. And may it reduce the suffering of other beings in the world."

Another factor, he said, would be the feelings of people he loves. "If I see that they can't stand to watch me suffer, I may make the choice to end it sooner."

So you believe people have the right to decide when to die?

Shutting his eyes a moment, he said this leads us into the area of situational ethics. "In the past, when churches or synagogues were the sole arbiter of people's morals, the leaders had no choice but to say, 'God gives life; God takes life; you have no right to interfere.' The hierarchy always has to go with canon law."

What's different today, he said, is that "every Jew and every Catholic are that by choice, and the hierarchy does not have the same control it had before. People who become pastoral counselors can go by situational ethics. They can ask, 'How old is the person? What is the medical prognosis?'" This is the gray zone, he said, where compassion can trump religious law.

But it's still illegal in most states to encourage or aid suicide.

"That's why I say you can stop eating and drinking. There's no law against that."

11

If You Go to Afghanistan

"You look troubled," Reb Zalman said as we settled in our chairs on the first Friday of August 2009.

Trouble didn't cover it. I'd signed up to go to Afghanistan in September on a peace mission organized by CODEPINK: Women for Peace. I'd never been to a war zone and never participated in a CODEPINK activity, but my attention had been riveted by reports that girls in Afghanistan were being attacked while they walked to school. Men would drive by on scooters and throw acid in their faces. Because they wanted to learn to read?

It had been eight years since the United States bombed Afghanistan, dislodging the Taliban from power, but conditions for women still appeared barbaric. President Obama was consulting with advisors to determine whether to send more troops, public opinion in the United States was split about the war, and I felt called to go and report the truth of what was happening on the ground.

There are moments in life when you make a plan and everything thwarts you: the flight is canceled, a storm comes up, you get a flat tire, and curse whatever prompted you to start on this venture. And then there are moments when you step into the current and it takes you. That's what happened when I was drawn to report on Afghanistan. Jodie Evans, a founder of CODEPINK whom I've known since our kids were in preschool together, invited me to join an eight-day fact-finding trip she was organizing for nine people in September. I would have to pay my own way, but I was confident I could sell a story after I returned. With only a month's notice, I thought it would be tough to find a decent airfare, but with one call, I was able to use miles to book business class seats all the way from Denver to Dubai. From there I'd catch a short flight on Pamir, the Afghan airline, to Kabul. Exhilarated, I started doing research.

A week after I'd booked the flights, a car bomb exploded in Kabul, killing hundreds. More violence was expected in the run-up to Afghan elections. Two *New York Times* reporters had been kidnapped, and the U.S. State Department issued a warning against travel to Afghanistan because of "an ongoing threat to kidnap and assassinate Americans." Suddenly my feet were skidding to a stop. What the hell was I doing?

The following Friday, when I sat down with Reb Zalman, I told him it's one thing to talk about death and strive to reach equanimity. It's another to realize you're throwing yourself into a situation where you might actually die.

Zalman nodded. "You can schmooze about it but that's not what happens in the gut."

"I'm not ready to die. And I'm even more frightened of getting maimed, losing my limbs or eyes, or having brain damage and coming home in a vegetative state."

Zalman suggested I consult an astrologer.

"I don't believe in astrology."

"So, let's see—what is calling you to do this?" he asked.

"I'm not sure, but something keeps pulling me to commit, and here's what I notice. When I think, Okay, I've set this in motion and I should see it through, every moment becomes heightened and precious. Like sitting here with you. Or hearing my daughter play Chopin, or seeing the aspens turn that astonishing gold. This could be the last time I hear my daughter play piano or see the aspens or talk with you, and how sweet it is."

Then I'll start feeling terrified, I said. "My whole body is shaking with fear—getting in the car, answering the phone—and I'll think, Why take the risk? I can't handle this level of fear. I don't have to go; nobody else will care."

I paused, trying to calm my breathing.

"So I resolve to cancel my trip, and for a moment, I feel relieved. Then depression sinks in, and everything seems flat and colorless."

Zalman gave a rueful smile. "You've decided to go back to the gray land rather than the one that's Technicolor, where everything feels significant."

That reminded me of Joseph Campbell's words about refusing the call. If the hero doesn't heed the call to action, he wrote in *The Hero with a Thousand Faces*, the "flowering world becomes a wasteland of dry stones."

"This morning, I was pretty sure I wasn't going, and I felt so bleak I had trouble getting out of bed. No amount of mental processing or meditating could help. When I feel that depressed, I don't want to live. I may as well go to Kabul! Is that insane?"

Zalman laughed softly. He said it's easier for him to

find equanimity at this point than it is for me. He just celebrated his eighty-fifth birthday and spent some time looking back over his life. "It looks like a beautiful movie. I don't sense that something is lacking or unfinished. When I ask, is there stuff I'd still like to hang around for?" He shut his eyes a moment. "I'd like to see my kids launched well and spend more time with Eve." He also wants to complete two projects: the conversations we're having about the December Project and a book he's writing on what he calls davenology—the art and science of Hebrew prayer. He's concerned that daily prayer may disappear from Jewish life, and he wants to write about how prayer is not merely reciting rote phrases but can be done in a way that transforms a person day by day.

"So," he said, staring at me through the red tortoiseshell glasses. "What does your unlived life demand of you?"

Is that part of the December Project? I asked.

"Yes. The unlived life comes to a person and says, I can't afford to die because I haven't finished what I came here to do. It demands to be heard, and it's important to listen. In my case, I do believe that I've completed the main body of what I signed up for. There's always more that could be done, but I feel I've done enough."

I told him I didn't think there was anything major I hadn't completed. "I've raised my children, had deep love, written the books I've felt called to write . . ."

"If that's the case, you're free to take risks. You can walk without fear."

"Easy for you to say," I blurted. "I'm mainlining fear right now."

Zalman shrugged as if to say, "Nu? What do you expect?"

In recent months I'd come to know that shrug—the *Nu* shrug—which invariably breaks my train of thought, stops it in its tracks, and makes me laugh.

"At the gut level," he said, "you won't be able to get rid of the fear so fast, but in time you will."

That was comforting—that the fear would gradually abate. And I also realized that there *was* something not finished: I was coming into a different relationship with myself. As long as I could remember, I'd carried a nagging fear that I'm intractably selfish and stubborn. I judged myself harshly and was ashamed of my flaws. I'd never had difficulty feeling compassion and forgiveness for everyone else, but it was only recently that I could begin to extend that tenderness and understanding to myself. "For the first time, I actually feel . . . lovely. Something is unfolding, and I don't want to miss it . . ."

"Ha!" Zalman said with a celebratory look. "It's the crone that's rising . . ."

I winced; I'd never liked that word. "It conjures up a withered hag, a witch."

"But in older cultures, it means a wise, revered woman," Zalman said. "It's the crown of age. Throughout history females have become wise when their nests were empty. They were able to see the panorama of reality from a much higher place. Becoming a crone is a beautiful thing."

Okay, I'll work on that, I said. "And I recognize there's something else unfinished. I want to see my children have children and be actively involved in the little ones' lives."

Zalman said it's important to have tendrils into the future, things you're looking forward to, or you may slip into what the philosopher Gerald Heard called involutional melancholia, an unbidden force that pulls you down to that wasteland of dry stones. "Your investments in the future—family, community, work—are lifelines against the melancholia."

"But isn't that living for the future?" I asked. "The spiritual teaching I've been trying to embody is about living in the present. Diving deep into the moment. Everything happens in the moment, not the future or past . . ."

Zalman nearly flew up from his chair. "I've heard all that, and I will march with a placard that says, 'Eckhart Tolle is full of shit!'"

Why would you say that? I asked. I'd felt enlivened listening to lectures by Tolle, who wrote the bestseller *The Power of Now*. "He's not the only one who teaches that . . ."

"I live in a larger place than the moment," Zalman said. "I live in a timeline, and I belong to a historic tradition. We have Abraham in the past and the Messiah in the future. If people did not have hope for the future, they would have given up a long time ago. The other day my body wasn't well, I was in pain, and if I just had the moment I would have wanted to die. Part of my moment belongs to my wife and kids. It's not just I and me. My criticism of Tolle, Byron Katie, and all those people is that they're only seeing the individual. It's spiritual narcissism!"

I told him I think the "now" they speak about is not a selfish state. "It's about understanding that worries about the future and guilt over the past are not productive and bring suffering. Serenity comes from being fully present and accepting what's happening now, moment by moment. And from that place one can be of service."

Zalman acknowledged that the Jewish tradition celebrates Shabbat, where you create a moment out of time. "But we are historic beings," he said, gathering steam. "We need to connect to past and future also. This is where Judaism is very good—with the concept of *tikkun olam*, repairing the world. That's why you're feeling pulled to go to Afghanistan. You're not obligated to complete the job, but you're obligated to do your part. Unless you can say that besides being in the moment, you're a cell on the planet and you have responsibilities to your family and your community, I'm not buying it!"

He sat back a moment, letting out a long breath. "Did you ever see me get so excited about something?"

"No! I never heard you say that anything is full of shit. I think the problem may be words . . ."

"That's possible," Zalman said. "Words are a serial instrument, and the mind is a parallel instrument. I can think two parallel thoughts, but when I speak them, it's a contradiction."

I could well understand the limits of words, especially when applied to matters of spirit. "I go nuts when Buddhist teachers say, 'You are nothing.' I am *not* nothing. I'm here, aren't I? If you prick me, do I not bleed? The larger truth I think they're pointing toward is, You are nothing and you are everything. You're formless and you're form. You're in the moment and you're in eternity."

Zalman nodded with enthusiasm. "That's where I go when I put myself in the presence of God. When I pray, then yes. There's nothing else. Only this connection, which is eternal."

After circling and clanging, we'd come round to the same place.

"Okay, Saraleh," he said. "I want you to live to 120 and be in good health. In case you decide you're going to Afghanistan, I'll give you something."

He walked to his prayer room, the dark cave with winking orange lights, and reached into one of his four charity boxes. He handed me a coin minted in 2000 that's worth one dollar and bears the image of a woman with a papoose—Sacajawea, the Shoshone guide for the Lewis and Clark expedition.

"The Talmud says that emissaries of a mitzvah [good deed] are not harmed," he said, explaining that I should keep the coin with me in Kabul and exchange it for one of my own dollar bills. "When you see someone who's suffering, you'll be my emissary and give them something."

I fingered the copper coin, which seemed to carry a kind of charge.

"And Saraleh," Zalman said. "I'll pray for you."

12

"Don't You Trust the Holy Spirit?"

As a young rabbi in New Bedford, Massachusetts, in 1955, Zalman used to rise at four in the morning to drive to Boston, where he was taking graduate classes in psychology and pastoral counseling. Arriving at Boston University at seven, he needed to daven, but Hillel House was closed. Most buildings on campus were shut except for Marsh Chapel, so he wandered through it, looking for a place to conduct his morning prayers. In one room he found a statue of Jesus, in another a large brass cross on the altar. At length he found a supply room that had no Christian symbols and did his davening there.

A tall black man—Zalman assumed he was the janitor— saw him one morning and asked, "Is there a reason you don't pray in the chapel?" Zalman said it was because of the Christian symbols. "In my guts and heart, it doesn't feel right."

"Why don't you look tomorrow morning and see if you'd like to say your prayers there?" the man said.

Curious, Zalman entered the chapel the next morning and found the brass cross had been taken off the altar and placed on the floor in a corner. He went to the lectern and saw the Bible open to Psalm 139, containing the words:

Whither shall I flee from thy presence?
If I ascend to heaven, thou art there. . . .

Of course, Zalman thought. When he finished davening, he turned the Bible to Psalm 100, a prayer of thanksgiving, then left the chapel and went to his class. In the days that followed, "this man and I were sending messages to each other through the Bible, and I still didn't know who he was," Zalman told me.

In the spring, he wanted to take a course listed as "Spiritual Disciplines and Resources, with Labs."

Labs? What would that be? He requested an appointment with the professor "to see if he was going to try to make a Christian out of me. If he was, I didn't want to take the course."

When Zalman walked into the professor's office, he saw the black man he'd assumed was a janitor. It was Howard Thurman, dean of Marsh Chapel, a legendary ecumenical leader who later would be a mentor to Martin Luther King Jr. Thurman offered Zalman a mug of coffee, and he explained his concerns. "I want to take your course, but I don't know if my spiritual anchors are long enough."

Thurman had an imposing countenance, with a high forehead and a bump of flesh protruding in the center. "It looked like a third eye that might burst open any moment," Zalman recalled. Thurman looked at his palms and turned them up and down, up and down, from dark brown to pink, again and again. Zalman waited and wondered, what was

Thurman going to say? At length, the dean fixed his eyes on Zalman and said, "Don't you trust the *Ruach HaKodesh* [Holy Spirit]?"

Zalman began to tremble. He hadn't expected the dean of Marsh Chapel to know Hebrew, and his question had struck deep. Setting his mug down, Zalman said, "I'll have to think about that." For the next three weeks, he brooded: Am I a Jew because that's what God wants me to be? Am I in the service of God, and if so, what do I have to worry about? But then, he thought: If I go to the labs and open my heart, will I be vulnerable? Will I be infected by Christian ideas? I'm a rabbi, a teacher; I have a family, a reputation.

Looking back, Zalman said, "It was as if I was afraid: I don't have a spiritual condom."

At the end of three weeks, he went back to Thurman and said, "I will trust the *Ruach HaKodesh*."

For years Zalman had been curious about other spiritual traditions. He never stopped studying Hasidic texts, but he also read Teresa of Ávila, Meister Eckhart, Ramakrishna, and Thomas Merton. In the 1950s he read *The Pillar of Fire*, a popular book by the psychiatrist Karl Stern about his passionate conversion from Judaism to Catholicism. "It made me furious," Zalman recalls, "and I wanted to run to the nearest priest and say, 'Me, too.'"

When Howard Thurman had asked, "Don't you trust the *Ruach HaKodesh*?" Zalman was catapulted into another level of relationship with God. "The screen was widened," he said. "From that time on, I couldn't see that reading or exchanging ideas with goyim was wrong. It was possible to know them as sincere servants of God, and I could learn from them." He was also beginning to connect

Hebrew teachings about mortality and the afterlife with those of other religions. The Jewish notion of the "world to come" could be compared to Catholic visions of purgatory and heaven, and the Hindu and Buddhist concepts of reincarnation were similar to Kabbalist teachings about rebirth.

Thomas Merton was a key figure in the evolution of Zalman's thinking. In the early 1960s, while studying for a doctorate at Hebrew Union College in Cincinnati, Zalman visited Merton at the abbey where he was cloistered in Bardstown, Kentucky, thirty miles south. Merton had read one of Zalman's essays and invited him to visit the Abbey of Gethsemani. Zalman took a bus, then a cab to the abbey, and had to ring a bell outside the gates by tugging on a cross tied to a string. Zalman stared for a moment, not wanting to touch the cross. He reached for the string above the cross and rang the bell. A monk who'd been watching said, "That's an interesting solution to a problem of conscience." In the evening, Zalman prayed he wouldn't die while at the abbey, so the Jewish Burial Society wouldn't have to come and pick up his body at a monastery.

Zalman had never seen a photo of Merton and imagined he would look like a Renaissance painting of a monk, with a hooked nose and dour expression. When Merton came out to greet him, Zalman was surprised to see a robust man with an infectious smile, "who could have passed for a college football coach." Merton took him to his quarters on a hilltop, opened cans of beer, and they began what Zalman described later as "a dialogue of the devout. I love God, you love God, so let's talk about how we're getting on with God and with our prayer."

They corresponded for years after that, which served to

"reinforce me in my Judaism," Zalman said. When I asked him to explain that during one of our Friday meetings, he closed his eyes. "A few days ago I went to a beautiful wedding where the ceremony was so sincere and deep. Watching it, I felt I was strengthening my own marriage vows." In the same way, he said, when he heard the monks at Gethsemani sing Gregorian chants, conveying a sense of peace before retiring, "I did my own evening prayers with greater fervor."

For Zalman, the borders had softened between Catholicism, Buddhism, Hinduism, and Judaism, as well as between his tradition and psychology. Not long after meeting Merton, Zalman read about Timothy Leary's experiments with LSD, which were producing the "sacramental visions" Aldous Huxley had described in *The Doors of Perception*. "I wanted in," Zalman recalled. When he visited Boston and met Leary, who was teaching psychology at Harvard, Leary offered to give him an experience of LSD in an ashram in upstate New York. But before taking the trip, Zalman went to Brooklyn to check in with the Lubavitcher Rebbe.

At 770 Eastern Parkway, men in black were milling about the corridors and meeting hall. The Rebbe was conducting a celebration, talking with followers, making toasts, and giving blessings. At one point, he looked around and asked, "Where is Zalman Schachter? The professor from Winnipeg? He should say *l'chaim*."

No one could see him.

"Maybe he's gone for a meditation, or a retreat," the Rebbe said.

Everyone laughed.

A student ran out to the corridor to find Zalman and

ushered him to the Rebbe, who gave Zalman a large tumbler of schnapps—strong alcohol. "One cup for the meditation and one for the retreat," he said.

"*L'chaim*," Zalman said and downed the first cup.

The Rebbe didn't respond with "*l'chaim*," as customary. Zalman figured he would say it after the second cup. But when Zalman drank the second large cup, the Rebbe's eyes looked distant, tuning in, it was assumed, to Zalman's past and future. The Rebbe shook himself and said, "*Nu*, so say *l'chaim*."

Zalman couldn't tell him, "I already did. You were spaced out." So he drank a third cup of schnapps. The Rebbe said, "Now for the retreat."

Zalman's cup was filled for the fourth time, and after he downed it, the Rebbe said with a warm smile, "You should have a good meditation and a good retreat!" He shot his fist in the air and when he brought it down, hundreds of Hasidim starting singing at the top of their lungs. Zalman's head was spinning from the schnapps, and soon so was his body, as he twirled, danced, and jumped like a being possessed. He believed the Rebbe was sincerely wishing him a good trip. But the other Hasidim thought, "The Rebbe is onto Zalman."

Weeks later, when Zalman was sitting in an ashram with Timothy Leary and the drug was coming on, he saw his Rebbe wishing him "a good meditation and a good retreat!" About fifteen minutes later, Zalman said to Leary, "This is better than schnapps."

13

Breaking Through Fear

I was buckling my seat belt on the plane in Dubai, just as the aircraft was about to leave for Kabul, when I thought I should take hold of the coin Reb Zalman had given me. I opened the zipper compartment in my wallet and was shocked: it wasn't there. *Be calm, look again, carefully.* I emptied all the contents out of my wallet and purse. No coin. I felt in my pockets and checked the floor. Nothing. Then I remembered. The night before, in the lovely Thai hotel where I'd stayed in Dubai, I'd taken the coin out of a compartment in my tote bag, intending to put it in my wallet, but I must have left it on the nightstand.

How could I! Zalman had given me the Sacajawea dollar because the Talmud said the emissary of a mitzvah would not be harmed. I'd promised to be Zalman's emissary and give the equivalent of that dollar to Afghans in need. Leaving it behind seemed a terrible omen.

As the plane sat on the runway, I called the hotel and waited on hold while they searched the room I'd just left. The engines began revving. Coming back on the line, the clerk said they'd found the coin and would hold it for my return.

Okay, I told myself, breathe, there's nothing you can do. The coin will protect you from afar, and you don't believe in omens anyway. Still.

Before leaving Boulder, I had continued flopping back and forth on whether to make the trip, until a week before the departure date. I was too frightened to go and I couldn't not go. A friend suggested I talk to a psychic she consulted in California, Andrea Davis. I'd never gone to a psychic, but I was desperate. I phoned Andrea, who asked what I wanted from our session.

"Clarity."

She said she was going to write three statements on three pieces of paper: Given everything, it's best I go to Kabul; Given everything, it's best I pass up this trip; I don't have enough information. She turned the papers upside down on a table, saying she would tune in to my soul's energy and let it guide her to the right message. She closed her eyes, shuffled the papers, selected one, and read me what it said: "It's best I go to Kabul." Andrea elaborated on what she was picking up: "There is no reason not to go except that you're afraid. Your soul says that fear itself is the issue, not Kabul. Your soul wants to go; this will open a new chapter in your life, and no harm will come to you or your group. It's not your time."

Come on, I thought, how could she know if it was my time? But the words rang true, not in the mind but as a knowing in the body, and hadn't Reb Zalman said intuition is more important now than thinking? Something in me knew that I should go and our party would not be harmed. Fear released its grip and from that moment, I felt calm.

I needed to prepare, though, for the possibility that I

would not come home. I revised my will and organized my financial affairs, which I'd delayed doing for years. I wrote a living will, spelling out the circumstances in which my appointees could tell the doctors to pull the plug. I did research on green burials and even made a "Memorial" playlist on my iPod—songs I wished to have played should there be a memorial service.

I wrote letters to my children, which was emotionally wrenching, and put them in the safe along with my will. When I asked my oldest friend if she would watch over my kids, I started to weep. That undid me, imagining I might be leaving them. "Don't worry, it's not going to happen," my friend said, "but if it does, your kids are my kids."

Our group met for the first time at the Dubai airport— eight women and one man—wearing, as we'd been advised, loose dark clothes that covered the head, arms, and legs. No tight jeans. We learned that all of us had arrived with the belief that the United States should withdraw its troops from Afghanistan and spend more money on development. Over the next eight days, our presumptions would be turned upside down, splitting us into camps with clashing opinions.

Every day we set out in a chartered bus at 8 A.M., returning late at night to sleep in a shabby guesthouse, far from the big hotels that attracted foreigners and were thus seen as targets for terrorist attacks. We met with Afghans from all walks of life, from politicians to warlords to refugees and NGO workers. We visited shelters for abused women, talked with soldiers at a U.S. army base, and sat in centers that were training adults to read. What startled us was that almost everyone we met, especially women, wanted U.S.

troops to stay and provide security so they could leave their homes to go to work and children could be safe walking to school. There was no way to get development money or supplies to the villages if the roads weren't safe.

Hearing this, some of our group still believed that troops should leave promptly, but one woman who'd spent forty years in nonviolent peace work reversed her lifelong stand, believing the military should stay and more troops might be helpful. "It shocks me to admit this," she said.

Afghans told us that if all the troops left, the Taliban would be back in twenty-four hours and would reinstate the ban on women leaving their homes for any reason—to work, go to school, or go to a hospital. They would make people paint their windows black so women couldn't see outside or be seen. The Taliban would also ban men from shaving their beards and everyone from playing music, flying kites, or raising parakeets, all three of which had been Afghan passions for centuries. In the garden of our guesthouse, there was a giant cage with hundreds of parakeets, who chirped so loudly we could hardly hear each other speak.

I was acquiring a humble understanding that, as one NATO worker said, "there is no solution on a white horse." I did not see how the involvement of U.S. troops could vanquish the Taliban and bring about an Afghan democracy. But I'd been moved by the bravery of women we met who'd received death threats from anonymous callers, warning that if they didn't stay inside their homes they'd be shot. The women continued going out every day to work on literacy programs, job training, and health care for women, and I was reluctant to leave them to the mercy of the Taliban. Our peace delegation was now split into factions that sniped at each other. The nonviolent activist who'd come to believe the troops should stay started calling those who disagreed "peace fundamentalists." The latter held to the line that any military intervention was wrong. "It's not our job to liberate women in other countries. They have to do it themselves."

As our departure day neared, I thought about the mitzvah coin Reb Zalman had given me and my pledge to pass its value to someone needy. At the start of the trip, our guide had told us that for our safety, we must stay with the group and not venture out on the streets alone. As a result, I did not come across anyone begging, and when we visited refugee camps where people clearly needed help, we could not give to one without giving to thousands.

The day we checked out, I decided to give a generous tip to the woman who'd been using threadbare rags to clean my musty room in the guesthouse. Our guide had suggested giving a few dollars, but I gave the equivalent of five. The cleaning woman looked overjoyed, singing out, "Tashakor [thank you]!" She held up the bills as if she'd never seen so much money. I gave the same amount, with similar results, to the waiter who'd served our meals and the clerk who'd helped us settle in our rooms. From their clothing and shoes, it was apparent they could use it.

Driving to the airport, we found ourselves trapped in the middle of a convoy of U.S. tanks and armored carriers. Something was wrong. Nothing was moving for miles, and this was not an auspicious place for our bus—a screaming target—to be stuck for an hour. I nearly kissed the ground when our plane landed in Dubai. I went back to the Thai hotel to retrieve Reb Zalman's coin, and twenty-four hours later I was home. Safe!

Zalman held out his arms with delight when I arrived at his home on Friday. I told him how I'd left the coin in the Thai hotel room but suspected it had protected our group from afar. We had needed protection. Ten days after we left the guesthouse in Kabul, it was attacked by terrorists in the early evening, while the two armed guards tried to defend the front gate. Our tour leaders had picked the place because it was deemed safer than big hotels. But that night, shortly after the attack began, a suicide bomb exploded, razing the building and killing almost everyone inside, including the doctors we'd met who'd come from India and Scotland to volunteer their services, and also, I feared, the cleaning woman I'd tipped. There but for fortune—ten days—went I.

"You'll never understand that—why you were spared and others weren't," Zalman said. He'd never been at ease with the fact that his uncle's family had died in Auschwitz while his own family had escaped.

I continued to carry the coin with me as I resumed my daily routines. It was supposed to offer protection, but the true benefit—the magic of the coin—was that it expanded my sensitivity and capacity to be generous. I remembered my mother had always given money, in small amounts, every time she received a request for a donation, and I began to do the same. I treated a friend to lunch when I learned that his employment contract had been canceled and he still had three kids to put through college. The amount, I was sensing, is not as important as responding, letting others know their well-being matters to you.

Reb Zalman keeps a stash of dollar bills in the ashtray of his car for when he passes people on the street holding signs asking for help.

"Do you always give?" I asked.

"Always, unless the light changes and I can't stop. Even if the guy is going to buy beer," he said, "why not still give?"

When I later wrote a blog about the mitzvah coin and how Reb Zalman gives, it drew heated comments. A doctor wrote, "Is it really a mitzvah to give an alcoholic money to buy more alcohol or drugs? He might commit a crime and hurt others. If you really want to help, why not give the person food or clothing, or donate to a shelter?"

Reb Zalman responded, "If you give a gift, it's none of your business what the person does with it. That's making a judgment. I never ask the person, why are you out here like this? The question for me is, do I turn away from the hand that's stretched out?"

I thought about the many times I'd turned away from street people.

Zalman lowered his head, looking in my eyes. At fourteen, fleeing the Nazis, he'd carried silver spoons in a rucksack to trade for food and lodging for his family, and when the silver ran out they survived by eating fish heads.

"Do you know," he said, "what it feels like to have to go beg?"

14

Kicked Out of the Nest

The idea for Jewish Renewal first crystallized for Zalman in the mid 1950s, in Starlight, Pennsylvania, when he walked out by himself into a field of birches and red oaks. It was the final night of the annual B'nai B'rith Hillel conference, to which Zalman, thirty-one, had been invited for the first time. Students and teachers had been meeting in groups, and on this night they'd presented songs and dramas. Most of the students, like the young people Zalman was working with in Massachusetts, knew little about Shabbat, keeping kosher, or davening, but they were yearning for meaning, seeking answers to questions that bothered them so.

As Zalman stared up at the black and starlit sky, he began to weep. "Dear God," he said, "these American kids have so little background, but they're hungry and they're good—they want to do right. Please, help me to reach them."

What came to Zalman that night was that he couldn't transplant Eastern European Hasidism, as the Lubavitchers were attempting to do, into this soil in America. "It would never take root," he thought. Zalman realized that what was needed was not to restore the religion of the *shtetl* but to renew Judaism in a way that would serve people in this time and place. "Renewal, not restoration," he decided. And that set him on the course to create a new branch—Jewish Renewal.

The landscape of the fifties Zalman was describing, as we sat together in Boulder, resonated with me, as I'd grown up then and couldn't wait to flee the Reform temple I'd been forced to attend. My family was not observant except on the High Holidays, when my mother took her mink stole out of storage to wear it to temple. The services were boring and Sunday school was torturous—a weekly dose of mocking and humiliation under a teenage caste system as harsh as that of India.

I was not interested in what I saw of the Orthodox world either. When I once attended *shul* with a friend from school, the very air seemed chilled and forbidding.

Zalman sighed. "The Orthodox made it so hard to get to God. They said: You have to keep 613 commandments and live a lifestyle that, to most Americans, was abominable. Like women having to shave their heads and wear wigs."

"And if you didn't know Hebrew," I said, "the whole thing was inaccessible."

Zalman said the language barrier was the first issue he addressed after that night at the Hillel conference. He went back to New Bedford and taught his congregation how to daven in English. "That leveled the playing field so everyone could participate," he said. At the time, the English translations of Hebrew prayers were stilted, not user friendly. Zalman called them "fake Episcopalian," with phrases like "blessed art thou" and "our father, our king." He started doing his own translations, using phrases like "You who are the source of life." He showed people how to chant the words in English, moving their bodies in rhythm as the Orthodox did when they davened. Zalman was becoming convinced of the importance of linking body movement with prayer. "That really helped people have an experience that was their own."

He also led guided meditations, which no one else in the Jewish community was doing. "I had no peers," he recalls. "Others looked at me like I was nuts."

There was one man who was on the same wavelength—Ray Arzt, the director of Camp Ramah, a Jewish summer camp in Connecticut. Ray not only understood but was excited by Zalman's ideas, believing he could motivate the young campers. He invited Zalman to teach and bring his own children to camp for the season. "He gave me a free hand to do whatever I wanted," Zalman recalled, "and the summers I was there, from '61 to '64, were my most creative years."

Reb Zalman let his imagination run, looking for ways to give the young people a direct relationship with God. While visiting Thomas Merton at the Abbey of Gethsemani, he'd been inspired by the scriptorium where monks were writing illuminated manuscripts. Zalman set up a scriptorium at camp, where kids could write their own mezuzahs. He gave each camper the Hebrew text of the Shema prayer and told them, 'Copy it carefully and show me what you've done.'" Then the campers would go to the craft shop, make a wood or metal cover for the mezuzah, insert the prayer, and fix it to the doorpost of their cabin. According to Jewish law as it's evolved through the centuries, Zalman said, it was not a kosher mezuzah, which has to be written on parchment by a qualified scribe. "But as far as the Torah is concerned," he said, "the commandment is to write the Shema on the doorposts of your house, and these kids had done that."

He also created a "tallisarium" where kids could make their own tallith (prayer shawl). "I went around to all the *schmatta* manufacturers in New York and collected remnants that had stripes on them," he said. He rented a sewing machine so the kids could come to the tallisarium, pick out the fabric they wanted, hem the sides, and use a grommet maker to punch holes in the corners. "Then I taught them how to tie *tzitzit*—the ritual fringes. After they finished, they couldn't wait to put on the tallith to pray."

On the first Friday they celebrated Shabbat, Zalman asked the cooks to turn their fans toward the windows "so the smells of cooking chicken would go through the whole camp." This created a delightful olfactory association with Shabbat.

Zalman taught the campers to meditate and created a private retreat in a cabin on the outskirts of camp. "Every afternoon at three, we took one of the kids down there with enough food for twenty-four hours, a tallith, a prayer book, a set of *tefillin*, and a journal. The next day we'd come for that camper and bring the next one in."

The most edgy step Reb Zalman took was with the girls between eleven and thirteen. Visiting a cabin of young women one evening, Zalman asked, "Have any of you had your period already?" A few hands went up, and Zalman said, "Is that something you want to talk to God about?" He wasn't sure how they'd respond, but the girls were eager to create special prayers for the beginning of menstruation.

Ramah was part of a consortium of Jewish camps, which shared the prayers that their kids had composed. When the young women's prayers were sent out, Zalman had to take cover. Directors called from around the country saying, "What kind of crazy thing are you doing?" Zalman responded, "It's something important to a young woman, and if we have a living relationship with God, they should be able to talk about that."

Many of the campers Zalman worked with went on to become Jewish leaders and rabbis, who said the spark had been kindled during those summers with Reb Zalman.

His experience with the young people was so rewarding that he began taking his ideas on the road. While teaching at the University of Manitoba, he would leave on most Fridays and fly to other cities to conduct his evolving version of Shabbat. "I had to be careful not to overdo it," he recalled. "You could bring in only so much new stuff." In Chicago, he led a service in total darkness, to intensify the experience. "We did dancing in the dark with God, so people should dance from inside, not for others to see." In Milwaukee, he ran a retreat for seventy members of a Reform congregation. Before the Shabbat meal, he told a story about a traveler who'd visited heaven and hell. In hell, Zalman said, the traveler saw a banquet table heaped with enticing food. The residents of hell had spoons tied to their hands but were unable to bend their elbows, so they couldn't bring food to their mouths and were starving. In heaven, he said, the traveler saw the same banquet table and the same situation, but people were feeding each other and were nourished. "So today," Zalman told the Reform group, "nobody's gonna put food in their own mouths." They sat down at tables and fed each other silently, re-creating heaven.

I asked Zalman, "Why don't you do things like that today?"

"We've gotten tamer," he said. "It was wild and woolly then." He said his mission had been to shake people up. "But the energy it takes to create that atmosphere, to bring people into it and hold the field so they don't start giggling or think it's crazy. . . . I don't have that anymore."

"How did people respond then?" I asked.

"It was always positive. They wanted me back."

As word spread about what Reb Zalman was doing, it was inevitable that his ties to the Lubavitcher community would be affected. In 1968, he was invited to speak at the Washington D.C. Hebrew Congregation, which had been founded in 1852, on land granted to them by an act of Congress. Zalman submitted two topics: "Kabbalah and LSD" and "Moses and McLuhan," comparing Moses to Marshall McLuhan, who coined the phrase "The medium is the message." The senior rabbi said he wanted both talks and advertised them for two successive Sundays.

By then Zalman had taken LSD with Timothy Leary, and the major impact, he said, had been a broadening of his views. "It was clear that what I'd experienced in prayer and meditation before—the oneness and connection with God—was true, but it wasn't just Jewish. It transcended borders. I was sitting in a Hindu ashram with Tim Leary, who was Irish Catholic, and I realized that all forms of religion are masks that the divine wears to communicate with us. Behind all religions, there's a reality, and this reality wears whatever clothes it needs to speak to a particular people. For Jews, it's a Torah with a crown. For Christians, the log-on to the infinite is Jesus. But no single point of view alone is right."

Hundreds of people mobbed the synagogue to hear Zalman speak. But one woman in the audience later attacked him in a Jewish newspaper, whose name he can't recall, and phoned Lubavitcher headquarters to ask, "Did Zalman take LSD with the Rebbe's permission?" The spokesman for the Lubavitchers said Zalman had done it on his own, and furthermore, "his rabbinic credentials are questionable." When Zalman read that statement in the Jewish newspaper, he said, "It hurt a lot." He wrote to the Rebbe asking him to clarify if and why Zalman's ordination by the Central Lubavitch Yeshiva was being questioned, but he did not receive a reply.

"When you're in the Orthodox world, you see everything through their frame," he said, holding up his hands to form a frame around his eyes. "But psychedelics had removed that frame. I could take on many points of view, appreciate many different religions and ways of dealing with consciousness." He said psychedelics had also given him a deeper appreciation of Hasidism. "The essential things I'd learned were confirmed, but by then, I was an embarrassment to the Lubavitchers." He sighed. "I was kicked out of the nest."

"You must have known you were taking a risk, giving that talk on LSD?"

"Yep," he said.

"You were willing to pay the price?"

Silence. Zalman's face looked somber. "I had to go my own way," he said, his voice falling to a whisper. "It was time."

15

Forgive, Forgive

O ctober is the bewitching month in the Rockies. The aspens, whose roots are all connected underground in one large tentacled family, turn a gold that's like no other. The leaves are not just yellow—they give off light. Whole groves flicker and shine, turning the mountains into living paintings of green and gold. Friends and I always carve out time to walk in the aspens, lie down among them, stretch out our arms, and take deep breaths.

Reb Zalman, however, in the shank of October, was holed up in his basement, going through boxes of old photographs. His task was forgiveness—a critical part of the December Project—and in the world according to Zalman it has three parts: repairing harm you've done to others, forgiving people who've harmed you, and most challenging, forgiving yourself.

Zalman wanted to connect with people he'd loved but lost track of. Going through photos, he picked out shots of women and wrote each a letter, telling them he was grateful for the time they'd spent together and asking if anything had been left unsaid or unfinished. He was concerned about how the letters might be received. "It would be nice closure for me," he said, "but the ethical question is, how would it be for them?" If the woman had changed direction and moved on since he'd known her, would a reminder from him be welcome?

In most cases he sent the letters, and "I got calls and letters back that were so warm, it was wonderful!" he said.

I told him I would like to do that also but was nervous. What if you still feel love for the person and don't want those emotions reignited? Or what if an ex-partner is hostile and you don't want to be verbally abused?

"I didn't have any angry partings with lovers," Zalman said. "In divorces there were angry partings."

"What did you do in those cases?"

He said there was tension for years after divorcing his first wife, but "toward the end, before she died, we were friends and called each other often to talk about our kids."

"I have an ex who's still enraged at me, decades after our divorce," I said. Zalman proposed that I write him a letter and say, "I send my warm wishes. I hope you have everything you want in your life, so when it comes to a close you'll be content, even in relationship to me."

I shook my head. "He's notorious for his talent at holding grudges."

"Then write the letter and don't send it—just read it aloud." Zalman said that in his experience this works. "Your thoughts will seep into his awareness, and you'll get some response—perhaps not directly, but you'll feel it."

I considered this but haven't done it, probably because I think there's no chance in hell that any positive wishes from or about me could seep through the barrier he's erected.

Then again, I thought later, maybe it's worth trying, maybe it would bring me closure.

I asked Zalman if he needed to do any forgiveness work with his eleven kids.

"I've got some unfinished business there." He said that during his first marriage, "I had to go kill chickens, teach Hebrew school, and leave at five in the morning to study for my degree. Yes, I didn't see my kids much, and yes, I paid the bills." In his sixties, he'd sent each child a letter apologizing for mistakes and asking forgiveness. "I got a lot of anxious calls asking, 'What's wrong?' They thought I might be dying." He makes it a priority now to spend time with them. One of the phone lines in his house, the "family line," has a number only known by his children and close relatives. When that line rings, no matter what he's doing, Zalman picks up.

We moved on to the second part of forgiving: people who have harmed you. Every night before going to sleep, Zalman says this prayer:

Source of creation, I hereby forgive anyone who has angered or hurt me, in this incarnation or any other. May no one be punished on my account.

"Is there someone you've had trouble forgiving?"

Zalman nodded. "One man—he was my poster guy for forgiveness." He explained that when he was a young rabbi, his *shul* was the only one in New Bedford that had a daily *minyan*, or prayer circle. People in the community who'd lost a loved one would come to the *shul* if they wanted to say Kaddish, the mourners' prayer. "Most of them would sit in the back, looking bored. I'd go up and ask, 'Would you like to put on *tefillin*?' They'd say, no, I don't believe in it." Later Reb Zalman would pay a condolence call and ask to see their *tefillin*, if they had them. "Most men hadn't worn them since their bar mitzvah and had forgotten how to do it." Zalman showed them how to wrap the black leather straps around the arm and forehead. "Once they knew how, all of a sudden they *did* believe in it," he said with a laugh. "What they didn't believe in was making an ass of themselves in front of others."

One stranger who showed up to say Kaddish had recently moved to town. After Zalman taught him how to put on *tefillin*, he began coming regularly to *shul*, became a member of the board, and eventually was named president. Then he fired Zalman.

"Why?" I asked.

"He thought I was not dignified. I drove a small car, and he wanted me to have a Buick. He wanted to be my boss, and I didn't want to be bossed by him."

Zalman was only eighteen credits short of earning a Ph.D. at Boston University when he was served notice that his rabbinic contract would not be renewed. He was preparing to write his dissertation but couldn't do that without a job to support his wife and five kids. He was offered one as Hillel director and assistant professor at the University of Manitoba, Canada, but it required an advanced degree, so Zalman used his credits to earn a master's degree and let the Ph.D. go.

He was still bitter about this when he devised the exercise he calls the Banquet for the Severe Teachers. "The idea came from the twenty-third psalm—'Thou preparest a table before me in the presence of mine enemies,'" Zalman said. "This man was enemy number one." Zalman imagined walking up and greeting him. "My dear man, *l'chaim* to you, and I thank you for kicking me out of the *shul*. If it weren't for you, I might still be a rabbi in New Bedford. Instead I went on to have a much larger life. So I celebrate you." And he raised an imaginary glass.

Zalman added, "It's really tough to forgive people who've wounded us. But in every wound there's a gem, just as an irritant in the oyster produces a pearl. The challenge is to find that pearl, something you learned, and say thank you."

I told him I don't want to wait until December to do this. "Forgiving is something we need to practice all our lives."

"You could say that about everything I'm suggesting for December," he said. "You could say this even applies to a baby beginning to suck. But right now, Saraleh, I'm in December, and forgiving is a top priority."

I was anxious to hear about the third part of forgiving—oneself. For years I'd been suffering from remorse about how I'd raised my kids. "I was strong willed and opinionated, and I didn't know how to set limits without getting angry," I told Zalman. "I got triggered and yelled. How do you arrive at the point where you no longer feel ashamed?"

Zalman called that kind of shame "high-fidelity regret. I don't think there's real fire in hell, but if you experience intense regret, that's what the fires of hell are." He said there's no point trying to dismiss or bury what happened. "But to suffer all the time is stupid."

"I just feel I wasn't patient enough, I wasn't wise . . ."

"*Nu*? So look what happened—you got wiser. You have

done a lot of shifting. And if you can't forgive yourself, bring it to God. You can say, I didn't comport myself well, but I've learned from the mistakes and I need you to release me now."

I was silent, imagining bringing this to God. Switching gears, I asked Zalman, "Did you ever have a crisis of faith . . . wondering if what you believe might all be wishful thinking?"

"Of course," Zalman said. "That's when the world looks gray and meaningless, and I'm a helpless piece of flotsam going down the tubes. If I try to push that feeling away by going to the refrigerator or watching a movie, it won't work. Better to lie down and go . . ." He sang out in a mournful baritone: "Sometimes I feel like a motherless child."

I was surprised he goes to such depths.

"Depressions do come," he said. "I get so tired of all the people wanting something, all the phone calls, and having to reassure everyone, 'I'm all right, I'm all right.' Sometimes the phone will ring and I'll have to answer . . ." He screwed his face into a smarmy smile and said in a fake cheery voice, "Helll-oooo-oooo?"

The look and tone were so creepy I had to laugh.

"In the worst case, when the depression is so dark I can't get up, I'll lie down and kvetch to God. That's what helps— talking to God about the misery. Sometimes I'll read the psalms, but it has to be done out loud, because reading a psalm with the eyes doesn't work." He likes Psalm 71, which he's translated himself because "King James is too fancy."

Please, when I get old
Don't cast me away. . . .

You've seen me through many bad trouble spots.
So come back to me, invigorate me.
And from the low depression lift me up.
Increase my sense of worth.
Turn to me and console me
so I can pick up my violin again
and sing to you, holy one of Israel.

As he recited the words, Zalman, like the aspens, seemed to give off light.

Closing his eyes, he said, "I ask myself, what is lacking now? I have a wonderful family, good friends, Eve and I are in a good place, and these talks about December are beautiful because they create moments of intimacy." He opened his eyes, and a current of warmth and appreciation moved between us. We always managed to arrive at this place, no matter how troubled or distracted either of us had been when we sat down.

Zalman said, "If I feel a lack, it's for fellowship, for peers." He's been caught in the crosshairs of both the Left and the Right. His former colleagues in Chabad can't understand why he's strayed so far. They say, "How dare you convey our secrets to people who don't keep Shabbos? How dare you talk to goyim? You should return to where you were. You can still repent—we have open arms." On the other flank, his leftist friends say, "We're universalists. You've been with us through psychology and mind-expanding drugs, why do you cling to outmoded laws and that antiquated Jewish symbol system?"

In every conversation, Zalman said, only part of him gets involved, and it's lonely.

"What about Eve? Can't you share everything with her?"

Yes and no, Zalman said. "The more you love somebody, the more you want to reassure her that she doesn't have to worry. So I sometimes say that things are better than they are."

He said the only one with whom "I don't have to be opaque in any direction is God. Here I find understanding in every way. The fact that I'm not strictly within the limits of orthodoxy doesn't trouble God, because He deployed me outside those limits." Zalman raised his arms and laughed. "Or *She* did."

Long after the Lubavitchers had kicked him out of the nest, and after decades of innovation followed by backlash, Reb Zalman decided to make a pilgrimage to Ukraine to visit the grave of the Baal Shem Tov. "I wanted to connect Jewish Renewal with its source, the founder of Hasidism," he said. Eve couldn't come because her mother was ill, so he brought his youngest son, Yotam, then twenty.

Zalman felt a kinship with the Baal Shem Tov because, like Zalman, he'd diverged from the dominant Jewish culture of his time. "In every generation," Zalman said, "there are people who say, 'These are the boundaries in which you must stay,' and there are those who say, 'I have to grow, I can't stay within the old skin.'"

The Baal Shem Tov, or the Besht as he's called, was born Israel ben Eliezer in 1698, in a poor, rural village that was part of Poland, then Russia, and now Ukraine. He never attended a yeshiva but was often found wandering in the forest by himself in a state of rapture with God. Legend is that he had divine revelations and was taught by heavenly beings. The rabbis of his day believed studying Talmud was "the highest of the high," Zalman said. The Besht did not reject studying Talmud but only the spirit in which it was done. He was quoted as describing a Talmudist as "a man who, through sheer study of the Law, has no time to think about God."

The Besht taught that God exists not just in the study house but in all beings and forms everywhere. He encouraged his followers to let go of their sense of separateness and join the individual self with the eternal divine presence.

For their pilgrimage in 2005, Zalman and Yotam flew to Kiev and continued with a driver to the village where the Besht had died, Medzhybizh (don't even try pronouncing that). The grave of the Besht was inside a two-story gray brick edifice. Zalman walked through the door and placed a note on the grave. "There was a tradition that if you stood there and sang a certain melody, he would join you and be your prayer partner," Zalman said. "I sang, closed my eyes and let go, and I heard something like: *Nu*, what is it you want?"

Reb Zalman interrupted the story to tell me, "We need to go easy in describing this, because it wasn't all verbal." He had a form of inner dialogue with the Besht, which began with Zalman saying, "We are doing Hasidism, but we're doing it in a different time and space. It's very hard for a Jew in our day to follow the narrow path of the tradition, and that's why I've been developing Jewish Renewal. But there are people in Hasidism who are holding the reins, and they won't recognize what we are doing. So I want to graft our tree to your trunk."

The response he received from the Besht was that Zalman had been called to do this work. The explanation given could be put this way, Zalman said: "There is a flow that moves from God to souls, that's given freely along with creation. And every once in a while there are people who want to dam up the flow, saying not everyone should receive it, only people who observe this and that. 'If they satisfy our requirements, we'll let them have a little.' But the flow gets narrower and narrower until they've built a whole dam and won't let anything through."

I sighed at the rightness of the image. I'd run up against that very dam.

Zalman continued: "What I heard from the Baal Shem Tov was: 'I had to dig under the dam so the waters could flow again. And you have done the same—releasing the water so it moves. In this way, you are my disciple.'"

I asked, Why couldn't I put this in the book?

"It wasn't a conversation you could have taped."

We both laughed. I'd already written the opening chapter and sent it to Zalman. "Remember," I told him, "I wrote on page 1 that I saw a comet in my bedroom?" I knew some people could dismiss that as a weird hallucination, and others might see it as guidance from a higher power. It didn't matter. I described it because the comet was a warning to me of the sand running out, just as Zalman's inner dialogue with the Baal Shem Tov was crucial encouragement for his work. Besides, I told him, as Hemingway once wrote about good stories, "They are truer than if they had really happened."

16

Friday Night Is Lovers' Night

The New Age was in flower when Reb Zalman started flying to Berkeley in the 1970s. The United States had withdrawn all troops from Vietnam in January 1973, and people shifted their focus from protest to cultivating gardens, exploring their minds, hearts, and bodies. It was the beginning of what Tom Wolfe would call the Me Decade. AIDS had not appeared, birth control pills were widely available, and *Open Marriage* by Nena and George O'Neill, which asserted that couples could have affairs without harming their marriage, was on the *New York Times* bestseller list and sold 35 million copies.

Reb Zalman was invited to San Francisco by leaders of the human potential movement to conduct High Holiday services for the counterculture. Zalman asked people to bring their little altars, sacred pictures, and meditation cushions. "You should have seen the room," he recalled. "There were two hundred people, the finest of Berkeley, with tie-dyed shirts and incense sticks." He led the services with prayers translated into English on an overhead screen, and when he sang in Hebrew, he urged everyone to sing with him. "If you don't know Hebrew, you can scat along—ya da da da da. But when I have my tallith over my head, don't bug me. That's when I really have to concentrate on facing God."

The days of awe with Reb Zalman had a universal flavor. The Sufi Choir came to sing, and on Yom Kippur, Cecil Williams, the pastor of Glide Memorial Church, preached a sermon on *teshuva*—the Jewish concept of returning to God.

The services had such a strong impact that people who were setting up the Aquarian Minyan, a new congregation in Berkeley, asked Zalman to be its rabbi. At the Berkeley group, women were counted in the *minyan*—the quorum needed to pray—and both sexes davened together.

There was also an informal tradition: every Friday night was Lovers' Night. "The hope was: no one goes home alone," Zalman recalled. They sang, prayed, shared a feast, and sang and danced for hours until "everyone was so high, who would want to spend a lonely night afterward? If you weren't there with a loved one, you loved the one you were with."

By then Zalman had married and divorced his second wife, the secretary who'd worked with him on his dissertation. He acquired a reputation as a skillful lover, and women in Berkeley were constantly hitting on him. "Could we have a date? Want to come home with me?" He said there was no element of debauchery or cheapness. "Every encounter was seen as a sacrament, a ritual, a path to attaining oneness. These were people I davened with, danced with, meditated with—people I admired."

Before a date, Zalman would have "union negotiations" with his partner to make sure they agreed on the terms. "I would tell them, we're not going to do any future tripping. We won't promise or expect anything beyond this time. But if you'd like to be my Shakti for the weekend . . ." He broke into a smile at the memory. "I would be delighted."

Always a great appreciator of women, Zalman brought the feminine sensibility to the forefront in his work. He was startled, then, when a woman in the Aquarian Minyan told him he was a male chauvinist. "How could that be?" he asked. When he next led a service and gave a teaching, he asked her to raise her hand if he said something chauvinistic. By the end of the talk he felt paralyzed; he couldn't say a sentence without her hand shooting up.

The problem, he realized, is that male supremacy is embedded in the liturgy, not just in Judaism but in other faiths. He made a point of replacing masculine words like "father" and "king" with neutral ones like "creator" and "source," but that was just the first step in removing male bias.

In 1976, he was invited to be on an interfaith panel of gurus, priests, and swamis, organized by the Sufi leader Pir Vilayat Khan. A man in the audience asked them if men should ejaculate while making love, or would that cause them to lose vital energy? As Zalman remembers, "It was all men on the panel, and they were saying, 'No, you should not ejaculate because it said in this text . . . rum da rum da rum . . ." Zalman signaled to the moderator that he wanted to speak. "You always go to the men," he said. "Why don't you ask what it means for the women?" The females in the audience broke into applause. "The deeper question," Zalman said, "is what happens on the spiritual level between the woman and the man when they make love, not what it says in the text."

Today, the majority of rabbinic students in Jewish Renewal are female. In the Orthodox community, which prohibits women from being ordained as rabbis, some justify the rule by asserting that when women become the religious leaders, men tend to drop out. I've observed that in spiritual groups led by women, the percentage of men in the room is small. "That may be the case," Zalman said, "but if men withdraw after centuries of domination, that's what's needed for balance."

A few years ago, Zalman gave a talk titled "Torah from the Feminine Side" on Shavuot, the holiday marking the revelation of the Torah at Sinai. He said most people interpret Torah from the masculine perspective. "It's the father saying, 'You must do this and never do that.' But when the mother speaks, she says, 'Use this as a model and adjust it for yourself.'" Zalman said that's also a prime distinction between the orthodox and progressive wings of the religion. "The orthodox say, 'These are limits,' and progressives say, 'These are models.' The orthodox claim the Torah can't be changed from the way it was given three thousand years ago." He paused, passing his eyes over the audience. "My point is: the Torah is given every moment."

17

When Mom Dies

"It's no accident," I told Reb Zalman, "that I'm doing this work with you. Death has been everywhere—in my face, eyes, and nostrils—in the last months." After I'd returned from Afghanistan, where the guesthouse I'd stayed in had been blown up, my mother died, then her partner of eight years died, then my sister's father-in-law died, and their family dog—beloved by everyone—developed cancer and had to be put down. I was still mourning the loss of one of my dearest, oldest friends, Woody Wickham, who'd died of liver cancer at sixty-six. He'd been the linchpin of a small circle of friends who'd been meeting to plan how we would live together as we grew older. We'd assumed we would die at about the same time—an illusion that had been smashed.

Before going to Kabul I thought I'd accepted the possibility that I could die there and had put my affairs in order. But I'd accepted this, I would learn, only in theory.

Two weeks after returning, I drove with friends to Steamboat Springs, to enjoy the fall colors and relax in the hot pools. I was out of cell phone reach for three days, and when we began heading home, I checked my phone and found a series of messages, increasingly urgent, from Terry in Hawaii. "Mom's had a crisis, her lungs are filling with water again, and she's having trouble breathing." Since Alice had arrived at the care home in Honolulu, her heart had been failing. We'd made the decision, following her own written wishes, not to give her extreme treatments but to let her go as gently as possible.

I told my friends at Steamboat I had to rush home and make arrangements to fly to Hawaii. It was only recently that I'd been able to experience unequivocal love for my mother. Most of my adult years, I'd found it hard to be in a room with her without suffering pain in my chest and trouble breathing. I fulfilled my duties, calling, visiting, and sending gifts at appropriate times, but it was always a relief to say good-bye. As Alzheimer's set in, though, and she became "pleasantly demented," her personality transformed from demanding and judgmental to sweet and happy all the time. She'd forgotten her discontent with me and everything we'd clashed about. I began to appreciate the gifts I'd received from her: a love of storytelling, curiosity, and courage. When I visited her, it was as if all tension had dispersed, like clouds giving way to blue sky, and we could give and receive pure love. It felt imperative for me to see her one more time.

In Steamboat Springs, we'd just ordered breakfast at Winona's, our favorite café, but asked to get the meals in takeout boxes. Driving home, sitting in the backseat, I ate the most delicious breakfast I've ever had: Eggs Benedict perched on a bed of fresh cooked spinach and plump artichoke hearts, with a comforting Hollandaise blanketing it all and sinking into a toasted muffin. Afterward there were cinnamon rolls that were warm and dizzyingly fragrant from the oven, covered with melting white frosting. I'll always associate that meal with my mother's passing. Every exquisite bite was mixed with stabs of grief and guilt—was it okay to savor food while my mother lay dying?

When I returned home late Sunday, Terry called and said mom had revived. She'd eaten dinner and was sitting up watching TV. When Terry handed her the phone, she said what she always said in the care home, even if we'd just talked five minutes before: "How wonderful to hear your voice!"

Getting there didn't seem as urgent now, so I booked a flight for Friday, but Tuesday night Terry called and said, "She's in transition, sinking fast. If you want to see her, come now." The earliest reservation I could make was the following night, but I woke up in the morning and it was snowing, in October! In the eight years I'd lived in Colorado, it had never snowed before the aspens dropped their golden leaves, but a three-day winter storm warning had been posted. Fearing the airport would be shut down later, I rushed there and told the agents I would stand by for anything that would get me closer to Honolulu. I caught a plane to San Francisco, spent the night in a fleabag motel, and took the dawn flight to Honolulu, praying my mother would still be conscious.

Terry, who looked exhausted, picked me up and drove straight to the home. She'd been carrying most of the burden and was relieved that I was there. Alice was lying in bed with her eyes closed, as they'd been the last twenty-four hours, Terry said. The gerontologist, Dr. Robert Gries, arrived and explained what was happening. "Her heart and kidneys are failing." We asked how much longer she might last. "Anywhere from two days to two weeks," he said. "When the kidneys fail, toxins build up and the system starts shutting down. It also causes endorphins to be released so she doesn't suffer. But she's not getting nutrition so her body is chewing up its muscles, and her lungs are filling with water so she feels like she's drowning. That's why she's struggling to breathe. She can't be her normal self."

Normal? What was normal now? I'd never been with a person as he or she was dying. I'd been told that everyone dies differently, but for our mother, it was like the reverse of birth. She had periods of thrashing and moaning and then she was calm, as if between contractions. The hospice nurse said, "It *is* like birth, there's pain and struggle to bring the baby in, and the same thing happens when leaving. It's a struggle. Our main concern is to keep her comfortable."

I remember thinking that she looked beautiful. Her face had a rosy color, and she had her withered arm bent up, with her palm to her cheek, like a bird with a folded wing. Leonard Cohen's "Hallelujah" was running through my mind, and I sang it with Terry, who'd brought her guitar. We sang every song that Alice loved, including a rousing version of "Seventy-Six Trombones," because when she had turned seventy-six, she said, "I'm seventy-six trombones."

She began to toss and flail, but when we tried to stroke her arm or rub her shoulder, she pushed our hands away. Terry, who'd been a hospice volunteer for years, thought her skin might hurt to be touched. I held out my hand near her palm and she grabbed it.

"Tell her that it's okay to go," Terry said. "When the

nurses come in to clean her, she'll open her eyes." As promised, when the nurses started sponging her with warm water, her eyes snapped open. I put my face close to hers and said, "I'm here, Mom. I love you. I'm so happy to see you." She stared back at me, and no matter what the nurses were doing to her body, she kept her eyes locked on mine. "You've been a wonderful mother," I said. "It's okay to let go now. Terry and I are grown; we have children, and everyone is doing well. You can just relax, let go into love. Love is waiting. Love is there." She puckered her lips, keeping her eyes on mine. "It's a kiss!" Terry said. Then Alice closed her eyes. Receiving that kiss was worth the frantic rush; it's with me constantly.

The next day, Terry and I were sitting near her bed, talking with the hospice worker who'd stopped by. Alice hadn't opened her eyes but had been thrashing more and tearing at her skin. "She's suffering," I said. "Can't we put her out of her suffering? Why prolong it?— she's not going back the other way." The hospice worker shook her head. "We can't sedate to pass. We can only sedate for comfort."

After she'd left, Alice started gurgling. I asked the head nurse, Preston, if the gurgling was a death rattle. No, he said. "It's just phlegm caught in her throat." I swabbed her mouth with a moist Q-tip and rubbed Vaseline on her lips.

My daughter, Rachel, who was twenty-four and working in Los Angeles as an intern in music therapy, called and said she wanted to fly in for the weekend. My mother had had a different relationship with my children—adoring and appreciative—than she'd had with me.

"But Grandma might be gone by then," I said.

"I still want to come," Rachel said. "I feel so far away, and I don't want to be by myself all weekend."

Dr. Gries came in to check Alice and wrote orders to increase her morphine. Terry and I were discussing whether
to move her to a hospice facility that was closer to Terry's
home when a nurse arrived and asked if we thought Alice
needed morphine now. We turned to look at her. "I don't
think so, she's calm," I said. Terry stood up and cried, "I
think she's gone. She is. She's not breathing."

We had missed it. She had passed without our noticing.

I went into shock. One moment, even with her eyes
closed, the life force had been there, restless, moving. The
next moment it was gone. The body was a husk, empty, the
eyes like glass marbles. All those opinions and pleasures and
pains and prejudices and humor and zest—gone. Where?
Where did consciousness go? Her mouth was wide open,
and I spread red gloss on her lips—she always wore lipstick.

We wanted to wash her body, which is a ritual in Judaism and other religions. We wanted to touch her with
love and care, as she hadn't allowed us to do before. It was
fascinating: the body seemed so tiny now, and it was so like
mine. I came from that body, I have the same body type,
and I knew it in my cells: this was where my body was going
in a short time—shriveled and hollow.

She'd wanted to be buried in yellow, her favorite color,
but we hadn't brought many of her clothes to the care
home. All we had to dress her in was a pair of yellow-green
sweat pants, a creamy satin blouse, and a yellow crocheted
cape. Nothing matched, and Alice had taken such pride in
putting her outfits together.

For the next three days I felt raw, removed from the
advancing world, sobbing at unexpected times and wanting
to be held like a baby. I had thought I was okay with dying,

but at this moment, it was not okay that Alice was a vacant husk, and it was not okay that I was going to become a husk. It's one thing to recite the words in Buddhist meditation, "I am not my body," and another to see up close what your body will turn into. I remembered visiting the monastery of Santa Katarina in the Sinai desert when I was in my thirties. Built in 530 AD at the foot of Mount Sinai, where Moses was believed to have received the Ten Commandments, it contained a skull room where the skulls of monks who'd died there over the centuries were stacked nearly to the ceiling, to remind current monks of their own transience. I had stared at the mountain of skulls through an iron grate and thought it ghoulish, like a Halloween display. But my mother's empty shuck brought the transience home.

We had a small family memorial for her at Terry's house, in which we all dressed in yellow and told stories that made us laugh and weep. Then my daughter returned to California, and Terry and I took care of arrangements. Alice's body had to be flown to L.A., where she and my father, who'd worked at Hillside Memorial Park in his last years, had bought caskets to be placed side by side in a wall. (Why, I wondered, do so many cemeteries have sylvan names: Forest Lawn, Elmwood, Rose Hill, the Pines?)

I'd just gotten off the phone with the funeral director, dictating the words to be engraved on the wall, when Rachel called from L.A. and said, "Mom, I'm in a store and I just tried on a bridal gown. I'm a bride! I'm going to be a bride!" She'd become engaged a few months before, but this was the first step she'd taken to prepare for the wedding. Seeing herself in the mirror in a long white gown adorned with lace and seed pearls had made it real.

Joy and grief swelled in me, all mixed up, as when I'd tasted the cinnamon roll with warm vanilla frosting while knowing that my mother was dying. When I described this to Reb Zalman on the Friday after returning home, he patted my arm. I could tell from his eyes that a story was coming. "This is from the Mishnah," he said. "Here comes a bridal procession. Here comes a funeral procession. The funeral has to stop and let the bridal procession pass. Why? Because . . . even when mourning, the priority must be on life going forward."

But when grief has a hammerlock on your chest, on your stomach, how do you go forward?

Zalman closed his eyes. "There is a Sara who has become fully enlightened and knows what her path in life was all about," he said. "She's not available to you at this point because you're in a dark valley. But she exists, she is there on a timeline we don't know, and she is your best guru."

Easy to say, I was thinking.

Zalman explained that no one can take a person to the ultimate understanding. "It's like the last move of the Parcheesi game I'm playing. Nobody can take me into that final free place but me." He added, with a smile, "So who is the one who is taking me there? The Zalman who did it already." He said he'll often sit quietly and consult with that inner Zalman, "and I get guidance from him. He is the better guru than all my rebbes, because he understands me more and doesn't want to push me to anything that isn't my destiny."

How accessible is this to you? I asked.

"As much as I give it time," he said. "The voice is very serene, you know? If I'm anxious about a problem and can't see a solution, it'll say, 'Come on, relax, it's not gonna be like that forever.' "

"How do you know it's not just mental chatter, or the ego talking?"

"The funny thing is, there's no litmus paper that can test if this is ego or if I'm just imagining it. But if my instinct is, 'This is the real juice,' then I can do something with it."

I asked if there were times he couldn't access the inner rebbe.

He nodded. "When I'm feeling like a victim, like a poor nebbish. Oyyyyyy!" He turned down his mouth and made a face like a crying simpleton. That made me laugh, and I was glad I could laugh.

"So," Zalman said, "it's not me or anybody else who can take you to the place of equanimity. But the Sara who's done it already, who's completed what she has to complete in life . . . She can show you the way."

18

Review Your Life

A new year, 2010, had arrived, and on the first Friday in January, I found Reb Zalman reclining in his chair under an afghan, wearing a tan knit yarmulke, tan slacks, and matching suspenders. He told me he was missing Eve, who was flying home from Philadelphia after attending the funeral of a close friend. He knew she would need some consoling, "and I also know that when I see her face, I will light up. Because the last few nights, being alone with the cats has not been the same. The day didn't come to the proper close if we didn't cuddle and have our talk before going to sleep."

They've been married since 1994, and their union marks the final resting point of a personal arc for Reb Zalman. His experience of relationships began with his arranged marriage in the Lubavitcher community, when he was nineteen.

After his second marriage, to his secretary, with whom he had two children, he found himself in Berkeley, where he was free to explore romance and sexuality with a variety of partners. He fell in love with one of the women he'd met there. They married, agreeing to have an open relationship, and moved to Philadelphia, where they raised three children while Zalman was a professor of Religious Studies at Temple University. They divorced after fourteen years, in 1991, and by the time Zalman met Eve, he wanted a monogamous marriage that would endure. "Monogamy was the sine qua non for us," he said. "We knew if we didn't have that, we couldn't build what we wanted, and I was happy with it."

Before marrying Eve, he said, "I was always hunting. That's how the male mind works. You see a beautiful woman, and before anything happens, you have her undressed in your mind. If a guy says that isn't so, I don't believe him. You're always hunting, but by the time I was seventy, that need had lifted. The whole business of hunting stopped, and there was peace in the heart."

He can still take delight in seeing young women in short skirts striding down Broadway near the University of Colorado. When he walks through the park near his home and sees carp mating in the stream, he'll call out, "Mazel tov," and sing, "Fish are jumping, and the cotton is high." But there's no urge to pursue or possess. Peace in the heart.

Looking back over one's relationships is a part of the December Project that Zalman calls life review. He created the exercise in the 1990s, and when I read about it later in *From Age-ing to Sage-ing*, I was loath to do it. "Just thinking about it makes me anxious," I said. I didn't want to relive all the times I made a hash of things, fucked up, yelled at my children, argued over nothing, married a man for the wrong reasons, and turned down a job that would have led to wealth and opportunities. Oy!

Reb Zalman laughed, saying it's best to do this with a

loving friend who can help you see how you've evolved, acknowledge what you've learned—especially from your mistakes—and forgive yourself. It's critical, he said, "because if you don't face those negative emotions and release them, they're going to haunt you some more."

He said life review has a different flavor in his eighties than it did in his sixties. "Before, some of my memories were like jalapeños—ouch! Now they're more mellow, like a cinnamon bun."

"That's impressive," I said, "turning jalapeños into sweet rolls. Can you give me an example?"

He said when he used to look back at his first marriage, "I would ask, why did I marry her? I did it to please my peers. Why didn't I ask my heart and guts how I felt?" It did not occur to him to ask if they would be well suited as partners but only if she could be a proper Hasidic wife.

Zalman had a beloved teacher who'd also been the *shadchan*, the matchmaker, who'd brought the couple together. "I would visit his home and find him studying Talmud, reading aloud to his wife, who sat beside him darning socks," he said. "I tell you, to me this was the idyllic picture! The scholar reading Torah to his wife as she mends his clothes."

Remembering that fantasy when he first did a life review, he said, "I wanted to kick that young Zalman in the ass! He was stupid. Now, time goes by, and I look back and say, no, be gentle with that boy of nineteen. Bring him a message from the future—he's going to be okay. And when I think about the children she and I had together . . ." His face lights with pleasure. "Everything had to evolve the way it did because of the lessons I had to learn."

Hearing this reminded me of Erik Erikson's description

of what he calls the final stage in human development, "ego integrity," the state one has to attain to be fully realized:

> *It is the acceptance of one's one and only life cycle*
> *as something that had to be and that, by necessity,*
> *permitted of no substitutes.*

This seems the equivalent of Reb Zalman's life review, in that both lead to acceptance. For Zalman, the first part is the "social review," reflecting on relationships and family. It should be followed by a "philosophical review," in which one asks, what has my life been about? What was my purpose? "I'm eager to find out what my deployment was about, and who was in my karass," Zalman said. "It would be falsely humble to say my life wasn't significant to Judaism. Look at the rabbis on that wall." He pointed to the rogues' gallery of men in fur hats and black coats. "I harmonized with their tune, but what's the larger symphony? I don't see that yet."

I asked if the philosophical review he did when younger was different from the one he does now. Zalman nodded. "When I was a young man, my philosophy was a line, a single strand that was the *one true strand*. Then I began to see other strands. Ramakrishna was doing something similar to what my Rebbe was doing, only for the Hindus. The Trappists were doing something similar with their prayer. And other strands came—from Native Americans, Freud, Jung, and transpersonal psychology. All of these have been woven together with my life experience so that now I see an intricate fabric where before I saw a thread."

Nothing reflects that fabric so well as the rainbow tallith Reb Zalman created in 1959. Up to then, prayer shawls had been black and white or blue and white, and in America they tended to be what he calls "prayer bikinis," narrow slivers of silk. Reb Zalman wanted a shawl that was more like Joseph's coat of many colors, enveloping the whole body. He designed it with the seven colors of the rainbow, corresponding to the seven levels of the Kabbalist tree of life. While visiting Montreal, he brought the design to a weaver of religious vestments and asked him to fashion what became the rainbow tallith. Zalman was still a Lubavitcher then, and when he wore that tallith to the Rebbe's *shul*, the man in charge of calling people to the Torah told him, "If you take off that *schmatta*, I'll call you to the Torah."

Zalman answered, "What you call a *schmatta* is what they're going to wrap me in after I've died. If you can't call me in it, don't call me." Today, people in synagogues of all denominations wear the rainbow tallith.

Zalman believes he was not the originator of the work he's done. "I was deployed to pick up wisdom from my tradition, blend it with many others, and pass it along. I feel privileged to have been used by God this way. But at times, I think"—he turned his eyes toward the ceiling—"how did you trick me into doing some of those things?"

You started a movement, I told him. "But for me, for many people, I would guess, it's not so clear what our life purpose was. What about those who feel they didn't accomplish that much?"

I read him a passage from *Caleb's Crossing* by Geraldine Brooks, a fictional account of a woman who lived in Massachusetts in the 1600s and at the end of her life asked, "Does any woman ever count the grains of her harvest and say: Good enough? Or does one always think of what more one might have laid in, had the labor been harder, the ambition more vast, the choices more sage?"

Zalman raised his palms, saying, "That depends on what standards you bring. There was something crucial and essential you had to do with your life, and you did it. If you had children, biologically you've served the world. If you've done something kind and loving for somebody else, you have served the world. If the blogosphere doesn't have you listed as one of the pioneers of the age, it doesn't matter."

I started to respond, but he motioned me to wait. "I know this is a difficult shift to make. In the past, when I received a book about Judaism, I would first look at the index to see if I'm quoted. That impulse is still there, but it has become less important."

Making that shift—from judging oneself by external achievements to focusing on one's inner development and heart—is something I struggle with daily. After returning from Afghanistan, I wrote a story I thought was riveting: how a group of women who believed the United States should pull out of Afghanistan had had their views turned upside down by what they encountered in Kabul, splitting the peace mission into two warring camps. I sent the story to every magazine, starting at the top of the hill and working down to tiny publications that few have heard of. I did not receive a single response. I couldn't even get anyone to read it. Eventually I broke the story into a series of blogs that were published on several websites, but getting the cold shoulder from traditional media was crushing.

I told Reb Zalman I was feeling irrelevant—I was an old-timer nobody wanted to hear from. When I was younger, all I had to do was call up editors, tell them what I wanted to write and they'd say, "Go for it." No more. I'd been aged out of the mainstream at the very time I felt I was at the peak of my powers.

"You think you're alone in this?" Zalman asked.

"No, it's happening to a lot of writers, because publishing as we've known it is dying. There are fewer outlets, and they often pay less than they did thirty years ago. Still, it feels like I'm getting the hook: 'Off the stage!'"

Zalman said he understood. "When I see some of my students doing better things than I could, I feel I'm a has-been. On the other hand, the elder mind is needed in the world, and our gifts will find a way to express themselves in a useful way."

I pointed out that his situation is different: when he gives a talk, hundreds of people show up to listen, and the University of Colorado has established an archive to preserve his papers, books, and recordings. "It's not the same as feeling your time is over," I said, "that things have moved on and you're stranded. Why am I still here? What am I to do?"

"Just sit with that," Zalman said.

"I've been sitting!"

"Saraleh," he said, "You don't see yourself from the vantage point I do. Do you remember the first time we met, on Long Island . . . ?"

"I remember taking a two-hour train ride from Manhattan just to see you." In the 1970s, when I was revisiting the Jewish tradition I'd walked away from at seventeen, I took the Long Island Rail Road to a synagogue in the suburbs where Reb Zalman—handsome and charismatic in his forties—was presenting a talk on Jewish Renewal. We sat together afterward, and though neither of us can remember anything we spoke about, we left an impression, one on the other.

"I had a sense, this is a person it pays to spend time with. It won't be a waste," he said. "I knew that you were a mensch I could talk and share with, and underneath, something traveled from my heart to yours and vice versa."

The words made me feel the way Robert Herrick described feeling in *Whenas in Silks:* "O how that glittering taketh me!"

Zalman clasped his hands. "Who said that people only make love with their bodies?"

19

Facing the Steep Decline

The plagues were upon Reb Zalman in August 2010. He couldn't sleep through the night, he had a tumor in his right eye and macular degeneration in the left, his legs were swollen from edema so he had trouble walking, and his heart and kidneys were challenged. I'd been away for a month and when I returned for our Friday talk, he said a medical intuitive had told him that if he didn't take action, one or more of his vital organs would fail within six months.

"Did you believe that?" I asked.

He raised his palms. "I knew I was not in good shape."

While he was brooding, an old friend called with compelling information. She'd been diagnosed with pancreatic cancer, which is usually fatal, but after detox treatments with a holistic healer, Adam Black, in Beausejour, a small town outside Winnipeg, Canada, the cancer was gone. She'd had CAT scans before and after the treatment, which confirmed that her pancreas was clear. Zalman called Black, who said he could help Zalman, but the treatment would be uncomfortable and expensive—he'd have to eat a large quantity of liver and stay in a hotel there for two weeks. Zalman sensed that Black understood what was going wrong systemically with his body, so he and Eve decided to go.

Of all the people I know, Zalman is probably the most open-minded about healing methods that sound woo woo. He'll try almost anything and evaluate the effects. But after returning from Canada, he told me, "It was the funkiest situation you can imagine. The guy puts me in a bathtub full of hot black liquid that's got all kinds of salts and clay in it and keeps pouring it over me." Zalman was then put in a tub of white liquid and when he got out, he said, he was standing up straighter and could see the bones in his feet, which hadn't been visible before because of edema.

After the second bath, though, and after eating more liver than he'd ever consumed, his body swelled and his skin broke out in sores that itched and bled, in places where, according to Black, there was internal infection or necrotic tissue. Blood oozed out of Zalman's knee where he'd injured it during a fall. The healer told him that blood wasn't flowing from his legs back to his heart because some of the vessels had collapsed and new pathways needed to form, which would take about six weeks. When Zalman flew home, he had to wear slippers because shoes were too painful. "I was miserable," he said. "Had I known . . ." He shook his head.

A few weeks later, though, he could put on his shoes and take walks again through the park every morning. He liked to give thanks as he went, praising God for the mountains, the lake, the sun and sky, and the treatment, which, overall, he felt had been restorative.

His energy was strong for the next few weeks, but on the following Friday, when I arrived at his house at our usual time, I found the front door locked. I rang the bell, then dialed his number. No response. I was turning to leave when the door swung open and Zalman stood there wheezing, trying to catch his breath after climbing up the stairs from the basement. He explained that he was alone that day so he'd locked the door.

He looked grim. "The decline is getting steeper," he said, waving his arm in a downward motion. The lymphoma in his eye was bothering him, so he'd had a CAT scan, which showed a new "suspicious area" in the stomach. A biopsy was done, but the pathology report was inconclusive, so the oncologist was sending a sample to the Mayo Clinic. "I'm in a kvetchy mood," Zalman said. "I'm tired—it feels like there's no helium in the balloon. If the angel of death were to come around now, I wouldn't argue with the angel."

He was distressed by the number of hours he was spending on body maintenance—doctor visits, treatments from alternative healers, lab tests, diagnostic scans, trying different diets, and swallowing gobs of supplements. "How much do I have to do?" he asked.

But there's always another voice in him that says, "On the other hand . . ." He conceded that despite the high maintenance required, he wants to stick around longer. "When I'm doing something I'm excited about—like teaching people how to daven with real feeling—I'm not inside the body checking symptoms."

The physical decline was like a shrill school bell—impossible to ignore—announcing the shortness of time. "There's also a wonderful, poignant thing," he said. "I'm treasuring the moments I have with Eve." But he wasn't engaging as much with other people and refused to go to events where there would be crowds or loud music. "I can't bear the noise—it's an assault on my body." He'd been at a cocktail party in New York and "the density of people wore me down. I had to take out my hearing aids and try to find a corner where I wouldn't be approached. I had to go like this . . ." He mimed putting blinders on the sides of his eyes, like those worn by horses.

He cut down on traveling because it depleted him. In 2009, he'd flown to Saint Louis for the annual conference of Renewal rabbis, but this year he'd asked if they could all come to Boulder.

Zalman could feel the loosening of his emotional ties to people. This was true even with students he'd ordained. "I can't describe how intimate it is to teach somebody, to give from your whole self," he said. "But now the person is launched, and I watch myself peeling off from that intense connection. My body needs to do that, and I trust my body."

"Even though it's compromised?" I asked.

"Hey, if I'd listened to it better, it would be less compromised." He clapped his hands and laughed. When he was younger, Zalman used to have open house on Shabbos when people were welcome to visit, eat, and pray. "These days, Eve and I have a private Shabbos," he said. Before Friday night arrives, he writes his love letter and slips it under her plate. On Saturday at dusk, they sit outside if the weather is mild and sing Shabbos melodies until it's totally dark. "It's so wonderful," he said, and I watched his body soften and his breathing become more relaxed. It was as if the words, like the smell of chickens roasting on Fridays at camp, had a Pavlovian effect, taking him to a Shabbos state of mind. The plagues, the tiredness, and distress had all lifted. For the moment.

20

Recalculating

I t happened suddenly: I awoke from a nap, swung my legs over the bed, and everything that's supposed to be stationary was moving—walls, doors, pictures, chairs. The whole room was revolving and blurred. I closed my eyes and sat still, letting the dizziness subside, but when I opened them again everything was still moving. I tried to walk but stumbled and had to lean against the wall, propelling myself forward along it, hand over hand. I remembered that my mother had complained of dizzy spells as dementia set in. Was this the onset of that, or a stroke or tumor?

When the dizziness persisted, a friend drove me to the doctor, who examined me and said it wasn't dementia, "it's a classic presentation of labyrinthitis, a disturbance of the inner ear."

Labyrinthitis? Really? I had the urge to laugh. That's how my life felt: running frantically through a labyrinth, round and round. The doctor said it could be caused by a virus or by small particles dislodged in the inner ear, disrupting the balance system. It usually lasts a week to ten days and then clears up. "We're seeing one to three cases of this a week in our practice," she said. I asked if the frequency had increased in recent years. The doctor nodded. "We're all so bombarded, we lose our bearings and have to learn how to live with the constant surge of information." She prescribed pills for motion sickness, which had no effect.

I canceled a canoe trip I'd planned for the weekend, canceled all my appointments, and stayed in bed. I couldn't drive, let alone paddle a rocking canoe. I was literally grounded, and once I'd accepted the situation, I took it as a warning. It was shortly before this siege of labyrinthitis that I'd seen the comet streaking across my bedroom, and I'd heard: That comet is your life, darlin', and it's in its final arc. Are you spending your days the way you want? Isn't that *the* Question, at any age? Are you spending your one and only life the way you want?

The next morning at Reb Zalman's, I'd told him that almost every evening, I sit at the computer until midnight or 1 A.M., writing, doing e-mail, looking things up, clicking on links that lead to other links until I've been ensnared in deep reaches far from where I started. I have to force myself to turn off the machine and go to sleep.

"Why do you keep at it so late?" he asked.

"I feel like I have to get more done."

He raised his eyebrows as if to say, *Nu?* "There's a driver behind you who's pushing you, all the time. But now that you've seen this and described it, the driver doesn't have claws anymore. He's been declawed, and you can set a new course."

Yes! I would set a new course. Recalculate, as the GPS in my car announces when I take a wrong turn: "Recalculating." I made resolutions: I would limit my hours at the computer and quit at 8 P.M. no matter what; I'd make sure to go out and see people at least two nights a week; and I'd check e-mail not constantly but only twice a day. I tried implementing the new regime but almost immediately started backsliding. Why couldn't I quit at ten instead of eight? I needed to check e-mail more often—what if a message was urgent? I was headed back to square one when my body blew the whistle, bringing me to a full stop. It was clear I needed to get serious about resetting the course and stop pretending there was a cornucopia of time ahead of me. I had an opportunity now to reflect and set priorities. When parents are encouraged to hold their kids back a year before starting kindergarten, they call it "the gift of time." This was the gift of time out.

I actually began to enjoy having a license to stay in bed, but the labyrinthitis did not clear up on schedule. Two weeks passed, then three, and I was still too dizzy to walk a block and couldn't swim without feeling like I was drowning. My internist performed the Epley maneuver to correct vertigo, but it didn't work. A neurologist ordered an MRI, and the results were normal. I'd learned that when Western medicine can't identify a chemical or biological cause for your problem, you won't find a solution in that arena. I began asking around for a good body worker who might help restore my balance, and all roads led to John Chitty, head of the Colorado School of Energy Studies. A slight man with thinning reddish-brown hair and an air of eager curiosity, he listened to my symptoms and asked me to lie on his table. Placing his hands on my temples, he said he was feeling for the movement of energy.

John asked what I wanted from the session besides relief from dizziness. I said I didn't want to continue rushing through every day, feeling frazzled and tense, but to flow through it taking pleasure in the moments. John said, "That's what this work is intended to do—reestablish the flow." He said the right side of my body was shut down, "no energy moving at all." I noted that my right leg felt inert, like a sack of sand, but as he moved his hands to different points on my body, the leg began to twitch involuntarily. I felt a longing to be held, comforted, and I heard: "It's all right to let go now." That's what I'd said to my mother just before she died, "It's okay to let go." Lying on John's table, I was conscious of a tight holding in my neck, jaw, shoulders, and stomach. I willed every muscle in each of those parts to unclench, go slack, relax. And then I heard: "It's all right to die. Not now but when it happens, it will be all right. Not dreadful or terrifying but easeful, warm." I remembered an image from a black-and-white movie I saw as a child, in which a man was sitting on the edge of a sickbed, telling a woman who was dying that it would be like being wrapped in a cozy blanket in a sleigh that was gliding through the wintry countryside toward a blaze of welcoming light. I realized later that there was no way he could know this; he just wanted to give the lady comfort as she passed. But the same image had come to me when I took a nasty fall skiing and had to be wrapped in blankets and pulled down the mountain in a sled by the ski patrol. I'd broken my collarbone and damaged my knee, but the memory of that movie made me feel a kind of well-being. When I remembered it again in John Chitty's office, I could feel the warmth and cheer of that final sleigh ride. I told him I was startled, I'd never sensed anything like that message: It's all right to die. Before going to Afghanistan, I thought I'd accepted that I might die there, but my mother's death had revealed how shallow that acceptance was. I'd accepted the possibility, the theory, but at this moment I *knew* that death would be all right in the way I knew that two and two are four.

Thoughts and memories came tumbling after: How the energy had departed from my mother's body. To evaporate into nothing? That was impossible, Robert Thurman, the Tibetan Buddhist scholar, had said in his workshop. "There is no such thing as nothing. You can't study nothing in the laboratory." I remembered John Donne's "Death Be Not Proud," and Walt Whitman writing in "Song of Myself" that "to die is different from what any one supposed, and luckier." Plus I'd been listening to Reb Zalman once a week for two years, expressing his confidence that "something" continues. There seemed comfort in the fact that every living being has passed into death. No exceptions. It's an extremely well-traveled path. "O! Death, where is thy sting-a-ling-a-ling? Oh! Grave, thy victory?" But it's one thing to read or hear this and another when the ting-a-ling sounds from within.

In his treatment room, John said that energy was flowing now on both sides of my body. My right leg felt alive, charged, as did my whole being. I sat up and felt a twinge of dizziness, but it was less severe than when I'd walked in. I knew I'd be able to find a way to navigate the years ahead in a different manner, instead of playing a losing game of beat-the-clock. But would I backslide in the knowing that it's all right to die, that this thing I'd been fearing and resisting is really okay? I was sure the experience would fade, but having felt it once, could I access it again?

I told John my thoughts, and he said, "Are you asking if that knowing has a shelf life?" I had to laugh, that's exactly what I was asking. "I guess we'll see," he said.

Reb Zalman looked pleased when I told him about the final sleigh ride. "Are you getting closer to sensing the afterlife?"

"I don't think so. Not in specific detail."

He pressed on, because he sensed it was his mission. "There's a job that the universe wants me to do, and I said yes. There's a certain yes, a strong yes, that's a response to: 'Do I want to be transparent to God? Do I want to serve the greater purpose?' My nos don't come from that place." He told me I wouldn't be working on this project with him "if you didn't have your own big yes. So let me ask, where does the no come from?"

It's resistance, and it happens spontaneously, I said.

He nodded. "An energy wall."

"My mind can't accept any description of the afterlife, whether it's Dante's, the Buddha's, or yours."

"May I speak to your mind?"

"Sure," I said, and sang the Carole King tune, "Where you lead, I will follow . . ."

"It'll be a pleasure," Zalman said. He loves to lead. "My dear Sara's mind, I think you have set yourself as a sentry. Would you please tell me, who are the enemies you want to keep out?"

Great question. As one of Reb Zalman's sons would tell me later, "He asks great questions."

"I think I'm protecting Sara, I'm not sure from what," I said. "I don't want her to get fooled, follow the party line, adopt a belief that may not be true."

"You are doing a good job, but can I tell you, dear mind, that I like this lady a lot? And she's curious and wants me to talk with her, but if you're going to get in the way it's gonna be hard. So could you please, in a heuristic way, just take what I say and try it, taste it, see what it's like? Would that be all right?"

"Absolutely."

Zalman pumped his hand in the air. "So we have permission."

"This is Sara talking," I said. "I have a vote, and I vote for the mind to take a rest. Stand down. It's behaving like the Japanese soldiers who kept fighting after their emperor had surrendered. War is over. *War is over, if you want it . . .*"

Zalman burst out laughing.

"I know that there's more to reality than the brain can fathom," I said. "That's a bridge I've crossed, but I have no idea what the 'more' is. I yearn to know, I've been a seeker most of my life, a seeker who has a skeptic's mind and knows that we can't know. That's the loop I'm in—I want to know, and I can't know. Is there a way out of the loop?"

Zalman skirted the question, as is his custom, and reflected on how Jews speak about the afterlife. Jewish prayers always refer to it as "the world to come," he said, "but it's a house without furniture. Since the 1940s, hardly anyone talks about it in clear language." Several years ago, Zalman had a student he was mentoring, Simcha Raphael, who was casting around for a topic for his Ph.D. dissertation. Zalman suggested he study Judaism and the afterlife, and they both immersed themselves in sacred and arcane texts on the subject as well as literature and philosophy. Raphael turned his thesis into a book, *Jewish Views of the Afterlife,* for which Zalman wrote the introduction. Zalman also studied what other traditions have said about heaven, hell, limbo, *bardos*, reincarnation, transubstantiation, psychic research, and near-death experiences. He studied paintings like those of Hieronymus Bosch, probing for the psychological meaning of those gruesome depictions of hell. He concluded that they're metaphors suggesting the disidentification that has to happen with the body, as well as with emotions and thoughts. After dying, he said, "there's going to be a shakeout cruise, and a lot of stuff will fall away." Zalman sometimes refers to this process as "the laundry—which prepares you to experience and understand reality, to hang out with great and holy minds, let go of duality, and merge back like a drop in the infinite ocean."

I asked if he thought there would be rewards and punishment—a settling of karma.

"I don't need my parents or teachers to appear and tell me, you did a great job. My ego might say, 'Hey, am I not gonna be paid off for the good stuff I did?' But what would I want for a payoff? That the Baal Shem Tov should come and congratulate me? That all the great *tzadikim* from the past and Ramakrishna should also come along and say, good job, Zalman?"

"You couldn't take that anyway. Nobody likes so much flattery. But what would a meaningful reward be?"

Zalman made a clicking sound, tilting his head from side to side. "Imagine if you would get a whole bunch of ahas, a flood of insights into why God did this and why things happened like that. We'd find out, how close did we come in our understanding? Right on this, not right about that. It would be like an enlightenment orgasm that goes on forever."

Sounds good, I said. "But I think I'd like to dissolve into infinite love."

"Be careful," he said, "with the ecstasy comes the agony."

"I guess my view is that it's all love, good and bad, everything is what it is, and everything is love."

Zalman said that's what happens in Lower Gan Eden—"You embrace everything in love. The flood of insights occurs in Upper Gan Eden."

"I think what you're calling 'upper' is the mind," I said, "and 'lower' is the heart. I don't think insights are higher than love."

"That's always a difference between men and women," he said. "Feeling versus reason. And you're right, if you go beyond duality there's no upper and lower, but then you're a drop in the ocean, and you think that's boring."

"True!" We laughed, knowing how each other's minds work and enjoying the jousting.

Zalman said he'd recently attained a different understanding of the afterlife, in which "we're all cells of a larger biosystem, and each cell has a unique function." He compared it to the way the human body works. "If the hand moves, it's because of the cooperation among the brain, nerves, and muscles, not because a puppeteer is pulling strings." In the past, he'd focused on individual people, what their previous lives had been, which commandments they'd fulfilled, and which they still needed to complete in a future life to attain realization. "I've given up that point of view—the thread of the individual personality. What I've been shown is: I'm a node of earth awareness and you're a node of earth awareness. The afterlife I can look forward to is that I'll be able to pour all my experience into the storehouse of the planet, so that human awareness can grow a little more."

Zalman spoke with passion about this framework: Instead of individual reincarnation, we're all part of a larger consciousness that's evolving. Every living being from the first amoeba that formed in the watery muck to the babies that have just been born are part of this consciousness and, on dying, will contribute to it what they've learned.

I told him I was happy this concept was invigorating to him, "but I can't go there with you. To me, it's another story, which may have metaphorical truth, may be pointing at truth, but doesn't land as literal truth, any more than Bosch's painting of tortured, burning creatures is a literal depiction of hell."

"It's so interesting," he said. "You're not into woo woo stuff, but you're getting guidance, you're getting messages." He sat forward in his chair, staring straight in my eyes. "I want to ask you: What is the source of the love you yearn for? The love you want to dissolve into?"

Another great question. I took a breath, letting the query roll around, and I knew, as with most spiritual questions, that there was no correct and unassailable answer. I felt . . . a presence, a quickening, a sense of inner movement, as when a door opens and a curtain flutters in the wind.

Zalman said, "You're going to know the truth. You'll see it like you saw the comet."

He walked to a shelf and reached for a box filled with small brass bells. He'd bought the bells on a trip to India, when he was looking for a tool to help him remember God. "It's a mitzvah to turn your attention to God—no action is required." He'd hung a bell in his car, he said, "and every time I hit a bump, it would ring and I'd say, thank you God, or, I love you God, or, I'm aware of you, you are One. If, God forbid, I should die in a car crash, my last thought would not be, oh shit, but a prayer to God."

What if you don't have a concept of God?

"It doesn't matter. Who or whatever it is that gives me breath and connects my synapses in a way that allows my heart to beat and lungs to breathe . . ." He smiled. "I'm so grateful."

He gave me a bell for my car, then raised his arms and sang, "The bell is ringing . . . for me and my God."

21

Let Go, Let Go

R eb Zalman was lying on a table, nearly naked and without front teeth, covered by a white sheet. Four men including a rabbi were washing his body, reciting words from the *Song of Solomon*. It was the *tahara* ritual performed on a corpse before it's wrapped in shrouds and placed in a simple pine box. Just as a baby is washed when it enters the world, in Jewish tradition, the body of a person who's died is washed and purified before it's buried.

But Reb Zalman was alive. It was one month before his eighty-eighth birthday, and he wanted to have a "practice *tahara*" to experience what it's like "to be a corpse." When he described it to me afterward, I asked what prompted him to take this step, which was unheard of in his community.

"Curiosity—it's part of my makeup," he said. It's also part of his makeup to break ground and bend rules when he believes it will serve the spirit. Because he's a *kohen*, a member of the priestly class believed to be descended from Moses's brother Aaron, he's not permitted to touch a dead person, so he's never witnessed a *tahara*. In coming to terms with mortality, he felt it was important to experience the ceremony, "so when it happens," he said, "I may be floating above, watching, and it won't be new."

To plan the ritual, he called on a friend who was a member of the *chevra kadisha*, the holy burial society in his congregation. Reb Zalman said he wanted to have the rite outdoors near running water. The friend asked, "Do you want us to put you in a pine box afterward and close it?" Reb Zalman shook his head. "Save that for the real thing."

The site he chose was a stretch of land behind the home of Rabbi Marc Soloway, running down to Boulder Creek. Rabbi Marc, 48, who describes himself as a "Conservative rabbi with Renewal tendencies," was shocked when he heard of Reb Zalman's plan, and said he trembled at the idea of performing the ceremony with a living person. "Then I realized, the whole meaning of Reb Zalman's life has been an embodied and experiential relationship to ancient rituals, so it made sense."

On a brilliant day in July, Reb Zalman arrived wearing sandals and black socks pulled up to his calves, black swim trunks, and a black shirt. "He looked as excited as a child," one of the participants told me. Rabbi Marc and three men from the burial society tied white linen around themselves and approached Reb Zalman, who was struck by how grave they looked. They helped him down the knoll to a secluded spot by the creek, surrounded by trees. After Zalman removed his clothes, dentures, hearing aids, and glasses, they lifted him onto a massage table and covered him entirely with a sheet.

Lighting a candle, Rabbi Marc led blessings, and another participant read from one of Zalman's books, *Fragments of a*

Future Scroll: Hassidism for the Here and Now. As the men gently rubbed wet cloths on his face, neck, and shoulders, they recited from the *Song of Solomon:*

> *His head is burnished gold, his mane of hair black as
>   the raven.
> His eyes like doves by the rivers of milk and plenty.*

Reb Zalman told me he wasn't thinking, "Oy yoy yoy, I'm dying. My emotions were amazingly calm, and I was puzzled—I wasn't feeling grief but serenity. Yes, this is what's gonna happen. This is how it will be."

He felt gratitude and love for the men performing this with him. As they moved on to wash his arms, torso, and legs, they said:

> *His thighs are like marble pillars on pedestals of gold.
> Tall as Mount Lebanon, a man like a cedar!*

Zalman relished the praise and honor they were giving to his body, although his hair had turned gray and his muscles were no longer strong as marble. Rabbi Marc said, "It felt intimate and awesome, seeing a man I consider one of the greatest souls of our time and who's been such an important teacher for me—seeing him so vulnerable and innocent. He was completely surrendering himself to our care."

After washing every limb, they poured water in a continuous flow down the length of him. Then they dried him, drew the sheet over his face, and left him alone for a moment. When they removed the sheet, a participant told me, "His face was just beaming, and he immediately started reciting the morning prayer, *Modeh Ani*, thanking God for returning the soul to the body. You could see how much he loves this world, this life, this body."

And yet, he was preparing to let go of this world, life, and body. I asked if the *tahara* had accelerated the process. He nodded emphatically. "I was saying the whole time: I let go, I let go."

The *tahara* was performed in a season when Zalman felt he was listening to the fourth movement of a symphony, "when you hear the music slowly, softly coming to a close." He couldn't walk the short path in the park without stopping to rest, and he had to take several naps during the day to replenish his energy. His appetite was shrinking, and he no longer could enjoy spicy food.

But he saw beneficial aspects as well. Recently he and Eve were sitting in the garden, watching the moon, when he felt "an inner expansion." Without trying, he'd relaxed into a state of no thoughts, no words, no agenda. Timeless peace. In the past, he said, he needed to focus with considerable effort to quiet his mind and body, and now it was happening spontaneously. This was due, he felt, to the most critical part of the December Project: surrender. "I've let go of all kinds of things, including ambitions. They've been fulfilled or somehow dropped away." He can appreciate just sitting, breathing the night air and hearing the swishing of a rainbird—"life in its most human, down-to-earth simplicity."

He used to worry about what would happen to Jewish Renewal after he died, but he's let go of that. "Most people wanted me to stay in the saddle as long as I could breathe, but I'd seen what happens when spiritual leaders remain in the driver's seat too long. People like Swami Muktananda and Pir Vilayat Khan—they were like kings, and when they died, there was a struggle for the throne, and their movements splintered."

For the past decade, Zalman had been letting go of the reins of Jewish Renewal, delegating roles to different rabbis. When he attended services at the congregation in Boulder led by Rabbi Tirzah Firestone, he literally took a backseat. "In the past I'd told people, 'I will not come into the room unless you all stand up, and you will not sit down until after I do.'" That was how his own Rebbe had been treated, and Zalman believed that if he wanted people to listen, they needed to show respect. "Now I don't feel that." He's been gratified to see that the rabbis he ordained are able to stand on their own. "The ship is in their hands, and I don't need to steer anymore." But along with giving up control, he had to let go of how he wanted things done.

As he began to yield ground, he said, "there were people elbowing and lobbying to be named my successor." He chose not to name one person but to create a list of twelve, "like the twelve apostles, people who've been rabbis and leaders in the movement. I want to empower them by giving them some royal jelly—some special teachings I haven't given anyone else. I'm going to write each a letter saying, 'I trust that you've got it,' but I don't want them to advertise that they've been named."

He makes a point of stepping back not only in public but in private. At a family holiday dinner, he recalled, "I was sitting with my whole rebbe outfit—the fur hat, the special chair. I gave a teaching, and after we danced around the table, I moved aside to let someone else sit in the chair, wear the hat, and lead."

Was there sadness in that? I wondered.

"I wasn't sad, but there's a flavor of poignancy, like music in a minor key. When I'm not at the center of action, there are pangs." I can relate to that. After working as a journalist for forty years, I feel pangs when I read about or watch a major news event on TV and I'm not in the thick of it, reporting.

"How do you let go of a strong emotion like sadness or anger if it won't leave, it has a grip on your body?" I asked. He said that setting your intention to let go is enough. "You don't have to know how it will occur."

Yeah, right, I thought. But months later, I actually experienced this happening. I'd been angry for weeks with a member of my family who'd been shunning me for no reason I could ascertain. This had pulled up a stream of events from the past, a nasty train of painful words and arguments going back decades, which fueled a rage in me that felt so bottled up it had to come out. I was making imaginary speeches to that person in my mind, diatribes that rolled on, gathering steam, until I realized what I was doing and had to say, enough! But the harangue would resume later, the same speech over and over. I caught it running through my head the afternoon of Yom Kippur. Okay, I announced to myself, as Reb Zalman had suggested, my intention is to let go of this anger. It's having no effect except to keep me tense and miserable.

Yom Kippur is all about forgiving—other people and yourself—and asking forgiveness from God. I attended the evening service with hundreds of others, and at a peak moment, we recited an alphabet list of wrongs we'd committed, patting our chests in a gesture of mea culpa, and then sang the *S'lach Lanu* prayer: forgive us, pardon us, grant us atonement. We alternated between reciting our wrongs (even if we hadn't committed those specific ones) and singing our prayer to be forgiven, and after the last round, Rabbi Tirzah cried out, "That's it. We're forgiven. The slate is clean."

I did not realize until I was walking to my car that the rage that had held me in its grip was gone. Totally. I couldn't find it when I tried. All I could feel was lightness and grace.

In a meeting with Reb Zalman months earlier, he'd said that there were other areas in which he was letting go. He was releasing himself from some of the formalities in his observance. "When I was younger, the liturgy made a lot more sense to me than it does now."

"I've always had problems with the liturgy."

"That I know!" Zalman let out a laugh. "My davening has become simpler. I have less stamina, so sometimes I'll just say, Dear God, look into my heart and see where I am. I offer you that as my prayer today." Zalman was inspired when he heard Gene Robinson, the gay Anglican bishop of New Hampshire, describe his prayer life in an interview: "I just sit and let God love me." Zalman thinks most people never sit long enough or are sufficiently comfortable with solitude to let God love them. So he sees December as the time when "you furnish your solitude with God."

"What does that mean—furnish your solitude?"

"All the beautiful attributes you feel—warmth, gratitude, love—that's furniture for the sacred place inside." He used to tell his students, "You won't understand prayer unless you set up that inner sanctuary. For instance, when I'm lying down to rest, I'll start my afternoon prayer, and it might not be verbal. I might hum or meditate or just commune with God." He especially likes what Rumi wrote, quoting the Quran, that God is nearer than the vein in one's neck. "I don't have to climb to the highest heavens to meet God," Zalman said. "All I have to do is go into that sacred inner place. So let's furnish it well."

He slapped his hands on the arms of his chair, signaling that the session was over. We made plans for me to stop by on his birthday, and I asked what I could bring him.

"I have all I want, I don't need anything more."

"What about an iPad?" I hadn't seen one in his office.

"I have an iPad. I also have a Kindle."

"There must be some treat I could bring?"

He closed his eyes and rocked back and forth, then shouted out, "Ha!"

"What?"

"A good Jewish rye bread. With caraway seeds, just a little salty."

"Really?" I thought I'd have to get a rye flown in from New York, since there's not a single authentic Jewish deli in the state of Colorado. Zalman said Breadworks in Boulder sometimes makes an organic rye. To me it's *goyishe* rye, but Zalman said, "If you can get one of those, I'll be happy."

That's another thing he likes about December—"You're free to indulge your appetites." I found that reassuring. When I was in my thirties, my women friends and I were always obsessing about what we could and couldn't eat and what we just ate and had to atone for. We decided there must be an age when we wouldn't give a shit about our weight and could pig out. Would it be sixty? Seventy? We longed for that day, but I was in my sixties and it hadn't come yet. In December, according to Reb Zalman, it's okay to indulge your appetites, and he urges people caring for elderly parents to let them do that. "People say sulfites aren't good for you. *Nu*? If I want to eat a frankfurter, it's gonna kill me? So?"

He recalled that when Aldous Huxley was dying, he instructed his wife, Laura, to inject him with LSD in his final hours. "When his doctor found out, he told Huxley . . ." Zalman imitated the doctor, folding his arms in disapproval. "I don't recommend it."

22

You Can Take Me Now

Follow the yarmulkes. The words played in my mind to the tune of "Follow the Drinking Gourd." Fol-low the yar-mul-kes. I was on my way to the ordination ceremony for new rabbis in Jewish Renewal, but I wasn't sure where it was taking place in the sprawling complex of the Omni Interlocken Resort in the Colorado foothills. First I had to decide which of four lots to park in. I spotted a man wearing a yarmulke leaving his car and parked not far from him.

This was Broomfield, Colorado, where a man wearing a yarmulke is not a common sight. I followed the one I'd spotted into a two-story lobby, where I saw more men and also women in yarmulkes, but they were not simple black skull caps. They were brightly colored, some like mosaics, satin or silk, knitted or crocheted, star-spangled or striped. Both women and men were wearing the rainbow tallith draped over their shoulders like capes. They made a colorful stream, gathering mass as they neared the doors of the ballroom, where four people were holding up a chuppah, like the canopies used for weddings. Inside the ballroom, about five hundred people stood up for the processional.

Reb Zalman walked through the chuppah first, using a cane and wearing an ankle-length black coat and black embroidered yarmulke. Then came the dean and faculty of the ordination program, followed by the ten who would be ordained: six rabbis, one cantor, and three rabbinic pastors. I've attended two ordinations, and what surprised me both years was how much gray hair there was. They all looked fifty or older, and one man rolled himself through the chuppah in a wheelchair. Unlike most ordinees at traditional rabbinic colleges, who are in their twenties, these people had already raised families and pursued other careers.

Rabbi Marcia Prager, dean of the program, walked to the podium and scanned the room. "To stand with colleagues in the presence of Reb Zalman, our teacher and founder, is a taste of heaven," she said. "Meet the ordination class of 2012."

Two ordinees took turns introducing the group. I started speed-reading the program, in which there were pictures of the ten and statements about why they'd committed to Jewish Renewal. Mark Elber, who grew up among survivors of the Holocaust, wrote that he'd wanted to become an Orthodox rabbi, but when the women's movement rose in the 1970s he realized he could not tolerate the exclusion of women from the Orthodox rabbinate. He longed for "a Judaism that combined the intensity and devotion of Hasidism" with progressive social and political ideals.

I turned my attention back to the podium, where a small woman with large brown eyes, Shayndel Kahn, was giving an oral collage of the group. "We stand on the shoulders of our ancestors and trace our family trees to Russia, Crimea, Poland, England, Romania, Afghanistan, and Germany," she said.

Mark Novak spoke next, saying that as children "we dreamed of becoming an archaeologist, a second baseman for the New York Yankees, three of us wanted to be rabbis, and one wanted to be Elvis Presley but later changed to Bob Dylan." They'd held jobs as an art curator, shoe manufacturer, Jungian astrologer, Broadway actor, bookstore owner, and pastry chef. "In 1969 one of us—he really did—attended Woodstock." In unison they said, "We are honored and humbled to be with you today."

People in the audience raised their hands in silence, wiggling their fingers at the ordinees. This is what they do instead of clapping. It made me think of Martians or other space creatures, who wiggle their fingers in silence to communicate approval.

Each ordinee gave a teaching on the Torah, in speech, poetry, or song. Many quoted from Hasidic texts, and in 2011, Shoshana Brown sang a *nigun* that had been a favorite of the fifth Lubavitcher Rebbe, Shalom Dov Baer Schneersohn, who died in 1920. After the song, she asked Reb Zalman if he'd "come forward and give us a teaching."

With high color in his face, Reb Zalman took the mike and faced the audience. He explained that the Rebbe used to sing that melody to prepare himself and his students for a transmission. "Want to hear my transmission?" he asked. Turning to the ordinees on stage, he threw out his arm. "*You* are my transmission."

Hoots and hollers came from the audience—no more silent Martians. Zalman continued, "Hearing people refer to one Hasidic master after another . . . you can't imagine what glee is going on in my heart." He felt like thumbing his nose at the Chabad people in Brooklyn "who don't have students who have delved as deeply and unearthed as much wisdom as you have today." He described the difference between a rabbi and a rebbe. "The best we can do here is to make you a rabbi. But we can't make you a rebbe—that ordination you get from below." He said that when members of the congregation ask you to arbitrate a dispute, "that's one thing. When they come to you and ask, 'How can I get close to God?' then you're a rebbe."

Reb Marcia began calling the ten ordinees to receive *smicha*, the laying on of hands in an unbroken chain that's believed to lead back to Moses in Sinai. When called, the ordinees said in Hebrew, *Hineni*, here I am, and called their teachers and mentors to stand behind them. When all had been called, there were three lines stretching across the ballroom. Reb Zalman stood at the center of the back row, his hands on the shoulders of the rabbis in front of him, who held their hands on the shoulders of those whom they'd prepared for this moment. The ordinees stood in front, eyes closed, as a wave of energy moved from hand to shoulder to hand to shoulder and out into the room. Everyone in the audience could feel the force of the transmission—a different experience from when Reb Zalman had received *smicha* in the Lubavitcher community. "I got a certificate and a handshake. That was it," he said. Onstage, Reb Marcia said, "In the name of Ya, the God of Israel, we appoint you as our delegates and emissaries, just as we were appointed. You are now ordained as rabbis and cantors. Your blessings will be our blessings."

Cheers and shouts of amen rang out as the rabbis threw their arms around each other. Driving home afterward, I felt infused with gratitude—I was mainlining thankfulness—

that the hundreds in that ballroom and the thousands in the communities to which they'll return are carrying forward the movement Reb Zalman founded, whose roots extend back through Hasidism to the biblical era. On the spiritual path, it's said that one can go deep or one can go wide—deep by staying with one master or tradition and wide by gleaning what's of value from different traditions. I've gone wide, but as a spiritual mutt, I'm indebted to the lineage holders who keep the original teachings and rituals alive so that those of us walking the wide path can take what we need and leave the rest. If generation after generation hadn't preserved the religion in its original form, we wouldn't be able to adapt it for our own time and needs. We'd find ourselves with a multitude of adaptations containing fewer of the original touchstones, and our culture would be impoverished indeed.

Reb Zalman has gone both deep, with Chabad, and wide, drawing from other traditions. He was made an honorary sheikh in the Sufi order by Pir Vilayat Khan. He once told a group he'd had his "Catholic period" with Thomas Merton, and he'd also had Hindu and Buddhist periods. The Jewish scholar Chava Weissler told him, "I knew you embraced the feminine, but I didn't know you had periods."

He's frequently asked, "Why be Jewish?" if truth is universal and the divine wears different masks for different cultures. After the breadth of experiences he's had, why does he hold tightly to the Jewish symbol system? In *Jewish with Feeling*, he wrote that Judaism, like every religion, is an essential organ for the health of the planet, providing certain types of wisdom the world needs, such as the notion of *tikkun olam*—fixing the world—and the right of every individual to wrestle with God. But on a deeper level, he said, "I feel that I made a promise. I entered a covenant with God when I was circumcised, and I can't see myself disengaging from the covenant that I believe gives meaning to life."

I asked him about an issue that comes up for me and others I know: the I-Thou relationship to God in Jewish liturgy. "I find that limiting, because it's dualistic. You're addressing God as the other. God and humanity are two, not one."

Reb Zalman said, "There are many ways of relating to God. I can pray to God as the other and, at the same time, know that nobody is separate. The whole shooting match isn't worth anything if I don't realize oneness."

At the reception following the ordination, friends and former students rushed up to speak with Zalman. He'd taken a room at the hotel so he could "hide," he told me. He said to the people clustered around him, "My battery is running low. Would you please let me go and rest? I can't be with you all tonight, but ask yourself, what blessing do you need in your life?" He paused for them to consider this, then said, "I ask God to fulfill that blessing."

It seemed 2011 was the Year of Zalman Appreciation. Two days after the ordination, another crowd gathered at the University of Colorado in Boulder for the dedication of the Reb Zalman Legacy Project, an archive of his work that contains 1,200 audiotapes, 500 photos, 60 books, articles, and pamphlets, and 50 videotapes.

In March, he flew to Ashland, Oregon, to lead a retreat organized by a rabbi he'd ordained, David Zaslow. On Friday, first the women and then the men gathered in a *mikvah* that had been created in a natural hot springs at the base of a mountain. Zalman recalled, "There we were, all men, completely naked in the outdoors, preparing to go to a higher level of purity. There were moments when I wasn't teaching, just davening along with everyone."

The last time he'd counted, Zalman had thirty-two grandchildren and fourteen great grandchildren, and at Ashland he met three generations of his spiritual descendants. Zalman had ordained David Zaslow, a spiritual son, who'd ordained a woman who was a spiritual granddaughter, who was preparing to ordain three people who would be Zalman's spiritual great grandchildren. "The sense of continuity I felt . . . you can't imagine," he said.

This was also the year that Zalman began reaping a different harvest. He'd been contacted by young adults in Brooklyn who were members of Chabad or other Orthodox sects. Zalman called them "refugees," because they were struggling with how to remain in their communities and also find the spiritual freedom they yearned for. "They want to daven with fervor but without tight boundaries," Zalman said. "They don't want to leave their families or change their clothes, but they feel like their minds are in a vise, and they want to talk."

"How did they find you?" I asked.

"I'm known in Chabad as 'the one who left.' They looked at my website and read a book I've written only in Hebrew, *Hasidic Teachings of the Fourth Turning*. They thought, this guy can answer the questions we can't ask our teachers."

Zalman had also written a sex manual in Hebrew, for yeshiva students about to be married, explaining female anatomy and lovemaking. "Yeshiva guys are so troubled,"

Zalman said, recalling how he felt before his own arranged marriage. "They've never been around women outside their family. Suddenly they're supposed to do it, and they don't have a clue." He sends the manual to people he trusts, but it doesn't get widely distributed. "If it did, there would be a fatwa out on me," he said.

After the "refugees" made contact with Zalman, he began teaching them on Skype. When in New York, he would meet with them in a progressive synagogue where they'd have dialogues, eat *cholent*, and pass around a bottle of vodka. "I'm so glad for this connection with the new generation," he said.

Though his body was growing weaker, and he still occasionally had bouts of despair, Zalman was enjoying a deeper fulfillment. His innovations that had shocked people in the sixties were now dispersed across the mainstream. Meditation and yoga were being taught in synagogues of many denominations, youth groups were doing the practices and prayers he'd created at Camp Ramah without knowing where they came from, and people were finding what he'd always wanted them to find in the tradition—spiritual fire.

This brings him joy. "When I hear a report that a younger rabbi in another city is doing something wonderful, something I never thought of, I'm delighted," Zalman said. "It's like a zap that can fill up the hole of despair, and it makes me feel I've been well used. For that alone, I say: 'God, I'm ready. You can take me now.'" A smile began in his eyes and moved through his body like music. "Any way you want me, I'm your man."

23

The Ultimate Letting Go

And where am I, after spending two years in weekly conversation with Reb Zalman? The divine seems more accessible, sometimes "as near as the vein in one's neck." If I close my eyes and breathe deeply, I often find I can be cozy with God, with Oneness, not stopping the mind but leaving it be and feeling Oneness lift me. The mind continues to question and find flaws, but it never succeeds in halting the seeking.

I try to follow many of Reb Zalman's precepts: trust intuition; when your memory fails, focus on your inner sense of presence—"I am"; keep your attention on the road forward, not the rearview mirror; be generous without judging; forgive—everyone, especially yourself; and practice letting go.

That last precept resonates like true north. That's what I'd heard lying on the massage table in a treatment room when I had labyrinthitis: "It's all right to let go." That's what I'd told my mother just before she died, "It's okay to let go." Letting go, or surrender as it's described in Buddhism, is the surest means to end suffering and bring about ease. But it needs to be practiced, starting with small things. This past summer, for example, while traveling with a friend, I wanted to take an evening flight, and she wanted just as strongly to take the morning one. I told her if I have to get up at 5 A.M., I'll be wiped out the rest of the day, and she said if she has to arrive in a new place in darkness, it unhinges her. I gave more reasons and so did she, and then I thought: Do I have to have it my way? Not really.

It's more challenging, of course, to let go of emotions like anger or grief. Strong feelings need to be respected and expressed. And then let go. It's not simple, but as I found on Yom Kippur, setting the intention is the way to begin.

The ultimate letting go—the subject that brought Reb Zalman and me together—is letting go of life itself. While there's no indication that this is imminent for me, the end is much nearer than the beginning. As the months go zipping by, like the flipping pages of a calendar used in old movies to suggest the passing of time, I've noticed that I'm more at ease with the reality of dying. I view it less with dread and more with increasing readiness for the loosening and releasing of ties. This is not a fixed position, of course, but one that's continually shifting, unspooling in a circular pattern like Reb Zalman's speech. The fear of nothingness—my personal terrorist—can still steal up and make me gasp, but at other times, the memory of that warm sleigh ride toward welcoming lights can bring a sense of all-rightness and peace.

When fear strikes, I like to listen to a poem Zalman created spontaneously when asked to record some inspiring words for people facing death. Lying down, he closed his eyes and imagined he was about to depart. He began by

...king God for being with him through his years, then said:

> It was a wonderful life. I loved and I was loved.
> I sang, I heard music, I saw flowers, I saw sunrises
>   and sunsets,
> Even in places when I was alone,
> You, in my heart, helped me to turn loneliness into pre-
>   cious solitude. . . .
> What a wonderful privilege this was!

He expressed his care for those he was leaving.

> I still have some concerns for people in the family,
>   for the world, for the planet,
> I put them in Your Blessed Hands.
> I trust that whatever in the web of life that needed me
>   to be there is now completed.
> I thank You for taking the burden from me,
> And I thank You for keeping me in the Light,
> As I let go, and let go . . . and let go.

Not bad. The last words, spoken in a rich baritone that slowly, softly fades, never fail to bring me with him.

And the afterlife? Has my mind been loosened, as Reb Zalman hoped? The truth is, I prefer not to dwell on what may happen after we die but to focus on the day, to drink deeply of the unique moment that will not come again.

When the time arrives, Reb Zalman has given me a model to aim for. I'd like to be able to embody the words he spoke that Friday in his basement, just before Passover, when I asked how the holiday feels in December. He told a story, of course, the story of when he was a kosher slaughterer in Providence and the chicken pluckers taught him the spiritual "Travelin' Shoes." He rose from his chair and did some dance moves. "I'm ready," he sang, "I got my travelin' shoes."

I'm trying on the shoes.

Exercises

Reb Zalman, Eve Ilsen, and I created these exercises to help you become more at ease with mortality. Taking up the December Project, Reb Zalman says, can make each day sweeter and more meaningful. It can also help you accept the challenging times and see their value.

We hope you'll approach this not as work but like Lewis and Clark's voyage into the unknown. Put aside all expectations, and prepare to be surprised. Try to approach the project with curiosity and a light and tender spirit. There's no right way to do this and no right or wrong answers.

First, set aside time and find a tranquil spot where you won't be interrupted. Proceed at your own pace, but don't try to rush or do it all at once. The questions merit reflection, so let them simmer. You can take up this project with a group, another person, or by yourself, but if you're doing it alone, you might ask someone you trust to be available if you run into troubled feelings or want to share an insight that delights you.

To begin, create a notebook, journal, or file on your computer for the December Project. Make a page at the beginning titled "Gratitude" and others titled "Forgive," "Things I still want to do or complete," and "Intuition." As you proceed, if you think of people you want to forgive or be forgiven by, add them to the "Forgive" list. Do the same with things you realize you're grateful for and things you still want to do. As you explore intuition, you can write notes on the "Intuition" page about how it came to you, whether you followed through, and what the outcome was.

With each exercise or question, we encourage you to write automatically. Don't think or plan, just write whatever flows without editing or judging. When you've finished, read what you've written and see what pops out, what feels like "the real juice."

Ready? Enjoy!

Exercise 1

----〇〇〇----

Give Thanks

A. Since gratitude is one of our most powerful tools, woven into every aspect of the December Project, let's start there. And why not begin each day by giving thanks? The traditional Hebrew prayer said upon waking, while still in bed, is *Modeh Ani*, which can be translated several ways, including this:

> *Source of Creation, thank You for restoring my soul to me, for the gift of being alive this day, and renewing me with compassion.*

You can recite this or your own version, or simply name three things for which you're grateful. But as you do this, pause and really feel each word or phrase: "Source of Creation," "my soul," "gift."

B. Take the gratitude walk, as a regular practice or spontaneously. It's helpful when you're off balance, but try it in different moods and situations until the thanking becomes habitual. You can do it anywhere—in a park or place of natural beauty, on a city street, or in your home. If you do this in a place where you've often walked, tell yourself: this time I'm going to thank every part of this path that has nourished me over the years. Reb Zalman and Eve like to walk by the lake near their home, giving thanks for the lake, the mountains, the reflection of the mountains in the lake, the smell of the junipers, the jumping fish, and the parade of wildly different dogs pulling their owners by their leashes.

It's easy to pay attention and be thankful when you're out in nature, so try it also in a crowded or unpleasant space, or when you're stuck in traffic—what can you find there to be grateful for?

You can also walk through your house. When Eve does, she gives thanks for the beautiful wood in the rooms, for a bed that's comfortable, for the chopping block that's perfect for cutting vegetables, for the miracle of running water—"You turn a knob and water gushes out."

A variation is to have someone take you on a blind walk through your home, which gives you a different perspective. Reb Zalman took a group of nuns on a blind and barefoot walk through their abbey, so they could feel the texture of wood and the warmth of carpet, the smoothness of stone, the massive heft of the altar, and the perfect proportion of the benches.

When you feel yourself overflowing with gratitude, turn your attention to God. We're going to use the word "God" in these practices, but feel free to substitute words that resonate with you, such as "Oneness," "Source of Creation," or "Higher Power." Give thanks in whatever form it takes that day: words, a song, a little dance, or laughing out loud.

Exercise 2

Make Friends with Solitude, and Create an Inner Sanctuary

A. At any age, but especially as we near December, it's important to spend time in solitude not doing anything, which is not the same as being alone, bored, or lonely. Solitude nourishes us and creates room for intuition and communing with God. So carve out time for solitude.

Practice looking and thinking from the heart. First, direct your attention to your head and imagine a line running from the front of your forehead to the back of your skull. Then imagine a line running horizontally between your two temples. Put yourself at the point where the two lines meet. Look out from that nexus point behind your face. Observe how you're constantly constructing a face, presenting yourself to the world—talking, smiling.

Now direct your attention down to your heart, and breathe into that space in your chest. Does it feel different from the place inside your head?

B. Create an inner sanctuary, a place where you can go to meditate or pray. Reb Zalman calls it "the place we go when we want to recalibrate our truth and our goodness."

Imagine you're entering that sacred chamber. Light a candle and look around. What do you see, do you hear anything, and how does it feel to be there? Begin to furnish that chamber, not with chairs and tables but with the qualities you treasure: warmth, gratitude, kindness, love. Feel each quality as it arrives, and let it radiate through your body. When you sense the chamber filled with light and love, invite God to join you. Reb Zalman calls this being cozy with God, who's not in the highest heaven but as near as the vein in your neck. Can you sit still and let God love you?

C. Feel the spark of the divine within you. Is it a tiny flicker or a flame? If you're unable to feel it, imagine that there's a spark and say to it, "Teach me, I want to know what's true." Ask any questions that arise, which can range from specifics like "Should I take this job?" to eternal ones, like "Does the soul live on?" and "Have I been incarnated before?"

Ask a question and wait. Don't push on to another question. Leave time for truth to seep in, like a puddle slowly filling with water. If the puddle doesn't fill in this period of solitude, let the question rest inside as you go about your life. Ask it again before you go to sleep. Don't worry. Somehow, some way, perhaps at the most unexpected moment, you'll receive a response.

Exercise 3

Meditate Between Contractions

As we grow older, our bodies experience greater changes than at any time since adolescence, and this process accelerates in December. Ailments appear that never struck before, and the decline can be steeper than expected.

When you find yourself in pain—physical or emotional—try meditating between the contractions. Picture a woman giving birth. When the contractions rip through her, all she can do is ride them, but in between, she can breathe, sip water, and remind herself that when this is over there'll be a baby. The pain won't last forever.

With physical pain, scan your body and note, in precise detail: Where exactly is the pain? How big is it? What shape is it? What color? Does it stab or pulse? Is it steady or periodic? Don't try to ignore the pain or squelch it. See if your whole body is tensing up, and if so, try to relax the parts you can. Take deep breaths and continue monitoring: Where, how big, what shape, what type? Often pain arises to tell us where the problem is, and when we give it our full attention, it diminishes.

Ask your body: Can you estimate or guess how long this discomfort will last? Remind yourself that as severe as it may be, it will pass. It won't go on for eternity.

Reb Zalman says that when he sees one of his children in pain, he feels compassion but knows that "it's their pain, not mine. I can't take it away. All I can do is hold a hand and be present." He says you can do the same with your body: hold a hand and be present.

With emotional pain, take the same approach. Observe and identify the specific feelings and physical sensations—sadness, pain in your stomach, rage—and be with them. Don't push them away or squash them. Say, "I know you're hurting, and it will pass."

Exercise 4

-----∞∞∞-----

Disidentify with the Body

Almost every religious or spiritual tradition affirms that the body is not who we are. If the body were paralyzed or amputated, the being we recognize as "I" would still exist. But most of us find it challenging to separate our identity from the body.

Practice disidentifying in small ways, when your body feels good as well as when it hurts. Imagine you're viewing your body from across the room or from the ceiling, observing it experiencing pleasure, pain, or a neutral state. When Reb Zalman's body is in pain, he addresses it: "Poor Zalman's flesh. You've been so useful, so dependable; you've carried me so well. I'm sorry you're not comfortable right now." That dialogue, he says, creates a wedge of separation so you can make the distinction: I am not suffering—*the body* is suffering.

Exercise 5

When Your Memory Fails

When you can't remember a name or word, where you put your glasses, or why you walked outside to your car, notice: Am I worried? Am I starting to panic or berating myself for being careless? How am I breathing? What story am I telling myself—Is this how Alzheimer's begins?

Take a moment to slow down and breathe deeply. Move your attention to your heart and ask: Do I feel consciousness, awareness, presence? Do I sense the field around me? Do I appreciate the singularity of this moment? Reb Zalman recommends that at these times, we connect with "I am. I exist. All the details I can't remember are not so important—they happen on the outside. *I* am here."

Somewhere in the world lies the object you've misplaced, and somewhere in consciousness lies the detail you've forgotten. Look about calmly. Wait a day or so. Tell a friend about it and laugh—the finest balm. You can search for the detail on the Internet, and if the glasses don't turn up, you can buy new ones or recycle an old pair. Know that almost every object can be replaced by another object. Take refuge in what's most important: *I am*. Even people with advanced Alzheimer's respond to love, warmth, music, and touch. "Something" is always present.

Exercise 6

Forgive, Forgive

Do you want to leave this earth with anything or anyone unforgiven, including yourself? Probably not. But while it's a crucial part of the December Project, forgiveness is a healing and freeing practice to do at any age. Every night before sleep, Reb Zalman recites the traditional Jewish prayer:

> *Source of creation, I hereby forgive anyone who has*
> *angered or hurt me, in this incarnation or any other.*
> *May no one be punished on my account.*
>
> *And if it be Your will, may I be forgiven for the*
> *hurt I've caused others and myself, and may I not*
> *revert to the old habits that led me to do harm.*

What this prayer conveys is that we are all as much in need of forgiveness as the people we're attempting to forgive, and most of us, out of habit, may take the same wrong steps again.

Since forgiveness has three parts, make three lists in your notebook: "People I've harmed," "People who've harmed me," and "Incidents I need to forgive myself for."

People You've Harmed

With each person on your list, begin by deciding whether to ask forgiveness in person, in a letter, or in prayer. It's best to do this face-to-face. Pray for the person before you meet, then speak from a place of humility and radical honesty. Acknowledge the harm you've done and that you regret it. If there's anything you can do to repair the damage, arrange to do this and follow through. If you're not sure what's needed to make amends, ask the person what you can do.

If it's not possible to do this face-to-face—if the person has died, is ill, or far away—write a letter. Imagine the individual sitting before you and read it aloud, so you yourself can hear it deeply. If you have any doubt whether sending the letter will be beneficial to the other person, keep reading it aloud every day until you sense whether you should send it. You may feel, after reading it repeatedly, that it's been transmitted. Reb Zalman says, "There's a field in which souls are connected, and any expression of or request for forgiveness travels through that field. People may be so armed that the message can't get through, but you've done what you could. Their psyche knows you have sent word."

If you've harmed people by speaking badly of them, spreading an untruth, or gossiping, this requires special action. The sages assert that harm done by speech is more serious than harm done by stealing or cheating. Money can be repaid, but the hurt caused by speech can't be undone. A Hasidic tale conveys this point: A man went about his community telling lies about the rabbi. Later, he realized he'd done wrong and felt remorse. He went to the rabbi and begged his forgiveness, saying he would do anything he could to make amends. The rabbi told the man, "Take a feather pillow, cut it open, go to the window, and scatter the feathers to the winds." The man thought this was strange, but it was simple, so he cut the pillow, went to the window, and scattered the feathers. When he returned to tell the rabbi that he'd done it, the rabbi said, "Now, go and gather up the feathers and put them back in the pillow. Because you can no more make amends for the damage your words have done than you can recapture all the feathers."

If you've said things about people that have hurt their reputation, their relationships, or their ability to do their job, write a retraction and give it to the people you told. Then ask forgiveness of the person you spoke about, understanding that there's no way to tell how far and wide your words traveled.

People Who've Harmed You

Are there people you have a tough time forgiving? I've heard men and women say, "What that person did is unforgivable" or "I can never forget it." What's important to know is: you have the capacity to forgive everyone. All you have to do is release the negative energy that keeps you bound to that person. You don't need them to apologize, discuss it, or see your point of view. You don't have to condone or forget what they did, understand it, see what in their childhood caused them to act that way, or become friends with them. You just let go—of the resentment and anger you're holding. Set your intention to do this, and keep reaffirming your intention until you feel yourself let go.

If you find this hard to do, notice: How does it feel in

your body when you're unforgiving? You're the one carrying the bitter seeds, which poison your system and under-
mine your well-being. Pretend you're letting go. How does
that feel?

Forgive Yourself

This may be the hardest practice of all. Reb Zalman suggests that you sit in a comfortable place, calm yourself with
deep breaths, and pick five incidents in your life that you
feel guilty about. With each incident, take yourself back to
the time, place, and situation you were in then. Feel any
stress, anger, or fear you had. Remember what you were
thinking. With the wisdom you've gained and have today,
would you do the same thing again? If you answer no, then
feel regret. Not guilt—try to keep that in abeyance. Just
regret. Then identify your motives and what caused you to
act as you did. Hold your younger self with loving care, and
forgive that younger person who didn't have the knowledge
and perspective you have now. Instead of calling your past
action wrong, understand that you had a need you were
trying to fill and that now you regret. True regret can loosen
the power of guilt.

Reb Zalman makes this distinction between regret and
guilt: Guilt is feeling "I have to pay the piper, and I'll never
be able to pay enough." Regret is, "I know I shouldn't have
done it, and if the situation arises again, I won't repeat it. I
learned from it and vow to do it no more."

When we were discussing this during one of our Friday
meetings, Reb Zalman said that guilt carries an expectation
of punishment. With that mischievous smile I'd come to

recognize, he said, "I'll give you a story." He told me that in 1956, before the Hillel Foundation in Winnipeg would accept him as their director, they insisted he shave off his beard, which was forbidden in the Lubavitcher community. But Zalman needed the job, and he complied. Later, when visiting the Lubavitchers in Brooklyn, he said, "I walked in there like a dog with my tail between my legs. A friend came up and cried out, 'Shame on you—you sold your soul for filthy lucre!' He laced into me for five minutes, then he said, 'Okay, enough? Now come and enjoy yourself.' He knew I was expecting to be shamed, so he let me have it and then said, enough! That helped me a lot."

Try this with yourself. Rant and excoriate yourself until you run out of steam. Then move on with life and enjoy it. If you still can't let go of your guilt, Zalman suggests, "Bring it to God. Say, 'I didn't comport myself well, but I've learned from the mistake and I need you to release me now.'"

Exercise 7

Kvetch to God

Remember Tevye in *Fiddler on the Roof* singing "If I Were a Rich Man"? He throws up his arms and cries to the Creator:

> *Lord who made the lion and the lamb,*
> *You decreed I should be what I am.*
> *Would it spoil some vast eternal plan*
> *if I were a wealthy man???*

We have the right to do the same. When Reb Zalman feels a depression so dark he can hardly move, he'll lie down and "kvetch to God. That's what helps—talking to God about the misery."

So let it out: all your sorrows, complaints, self-pity, anguish, how you just can't take it anymore! When it's all been voiced and you're spent, lie or sit quietly. Turn your attention to gratitude. If necessary, force yourself to come up with things you're grateful for: fingers that work, teeth that can chew, a car that carries you, a comfortable chair that supports your back . . . Then smile, even if you're faking it, because smiling releases endorphins. Open yourself to presence, to receiving love. Imagine the warmth traveling through your veins, bathing every cell.

If you still feel stuck in darkness, go back and kvetch some more.

Exercise 8

Make Room for Intuition

Reb Zalman says in the December years intuition is more important than thinking, and we need to nurture our ability to receive it. Direct your attention into your heart space, and listen for what Reb Zalman calls "the one who's done it already," the realized self, who knows and accepts you with boundless compassion. You may hear what seems like a random thought, or you may pose a question and receive a response—in words, an image, or a feeling. How can you tell if it's just activity of the brain or if it's guidance?

One way is to lean into what you hear—start to implement the guidance and see what happens. In 2009, I felt a pull to go to Afghanistan but wasn't sure why. I began making inquiries, and immediately I found a group scheduled to go there on a peace mission and was able to use airline miles to purchase tickets.

You've probably had times when you make a plan and a dozen roadblocks pop up. Then there are times when everything aligns to support you. If things flow, as they did for my trip to Kabul, that's a good indication that you're probably following guidance.

Practice listening for intuition about small things, which have relatively small consequences. Ask a question like, should I go here or there for lunch? Listen to the first impulse that arises and pay attention to how it comes: a voice, a word, an image on the side of a passing bus? How did you feel when you heard, saw, or sensed it? Did you follow through, and what were the results?

Keep notes on your Intuition page and, after a time, look for patterns. Can you tell what the voice of intuition is for you, as opposed to, say, your mother's voice or your ego's preference? If you lean into what you receive, you'll begin to get a sense of when it's the real juice.

Exercise 9

------ ◦◦◦◦ ------

Review Your Life

The Social Review

In your notebook, take each decade and list the key people with whom you were involved. Start with your family and the first friends you made. What did you have in common, and how did they influence you? Thank them all for their contributions.

As you proceed through your teens, twenties, thirties, and on, identify the key relationships. What were the gifts, where was the tension, and how did they prepare you for what came next?

This exercise may show you people with whom you need to do forgiveness work. If there was unfinished business, write a letter and perhaps include a photo from that time. Read the letter aloud and decide if it's appropriate to mail it, or just envision the person and express the truth to him or her.

In your notebook, describe what in each decade you're thankful for and what you feel was a mistake. Can you see what you learned from that mistake and why it had to happen as it did?

When you come to the present decade, look over the whole picture. Try to see the patterns and how you've evolved. Is there a thread, a fine gold thread that runs through all the pieces and ties them together? What is that thread?

The Philosophical Review

This is where you explore what your purpose was, what your life has been about. What were the key lessons you may have come here to work on? This review may be daunting, and ideally you should do it with someone who unquestionably loves you and can help you sort through the murk and find the pearls.

Again, take one decade at a time and identify what you're proud of. What were your achievements, and what were the most valuable teachings? If a memory makes you wince with remorse, do the forgiveness exercise. Take yourself back to the time the incident occurred and comfort your younger self, bringing a message from the future: All will be well. All will be well.

Imagine you're with your children or, if you don't have children, with close relatives or friends. Imagine them asking what was most important in your life? What was your unique contribution? Write your answer.

If this doesn't seem the optimum time for life review, Reb Zalman suggests starting a weekly review, as he does every Shabbat. When Friday evening comes, look back over the week and write down what gave you joy, what gave you trouble, and what you learned. Creating a habit of doing this weekly will make it easier to look back over larger chunks of time and, eventually, to scan the full picture. Seeing that picture with clear eyes can bring fulfillment, serenity, and readiness to let go.

Exercise 10

―――∞――――

Claim Your Unlived Life

Imagine feeling so complete with your life that if, at any moment, the Angel of Death were to call for you, you could drop everything and follow the angel into the Unknown.
Now look at your life as it is in this moment. What is urgent that you still need to do before you can feel complete and free to follow that angel? Say to yourself, "I can't die now because I haven't . . ."

Make a distinction between what you urgently need to do and what you would like to do, and write them in two separate lists. An example of the first would be: secure funding for our organization so it can continue to thrive. An example of the second: see my children marry and have children. Notice what you have the means to do and what is beyond your control.

With the first list of urgent needs, if possible, enlist the aid of a friend or counselor in planning how to accomplish them. With the second list, make those items a priority in your current life. Dedicate more time to being with children and family if that's what you feel would be incomplete.

Another tool to clarify your priorities is to ask yourself: If you *knew* the world were going to end in three days, what would you do? Write what comes to you. Then ask, are you doing that now, and doing it enough?

Exercise 11

⟨⟨⟨⟩⟩⟩

Hang a Bell

Hang a small bell in your car, perhaps on the rearview mirror, so that it rings when you hit a bump in the road. Or attach the bell to a door in your house that you often walk through. Choose a short phrase to say when you hear the bell that reminds you: there's more to this moment than getting on with your next task. Reb Zalman says it's a mitzvah to turn your attention to God. So when the bell rings, he says, "Thank you God," or "You are One."

Allow the bell and the phrase to shift you for a moment out of your daily routine, and into gratitude and awareness of the greater picture.

Exercise 12

~~∞~~

Let Go

A. Practice letting go, or surrender, by accepting each small event in your day. Let go of your attachment to how it should happen and to judging if it's good or bad. See if you can accept what is, moment by moment. The sky is gray, the coffee is strong, your friend is calling to reschedule a plan. Make a list of what you can't accept and write down what stands between you and acceptance.

B. Practice dying—the ultimate letting go. When Plato, at the end of his life, was asked to sum up his philosophy, he said, "Practice dying." I suspect what he meant was to practice dying to the past, dying to the known, and opening your arms to the unknown. Reb Zalman used to practice dying on the subway each day when he was a yeshiva student, saying, "When I reach the Atlantic Avenue station I'll be gone. So let me say the Shema."

Try imagining that at a certain point in your day, you'll be gone. What's important to do in your last moments? Notice if this heightens your appreciation of the day and inspires you to give yourself completely to it.

C. Put your financial affairs and end-of-life issues in order. Make sure you have an up-to-date will, a trust for your descendants, if appropriate, a living will stating your wishes about extreme medical treatments, a power of attorney and medical power of attorney. Write letters to your children to be opened after you die. Compose an emergency list, stating your blood type and allergies, your loved ones and friends to be contacted, your doctors, attorney, and accountant, your financial accounts, credit cards, and insurance information, where your important documents are stored, and how you'd like your remains to be disposed.

It's also important to write how you wish to be cared for if you become unable to make decisions. I did this before leaving for Afghanistan, writing that I want to be cared for in my own home, with music played and books read to me, and to be taken outdoors in nature. I concluded, "I would like to be as conscious and aware about the dying process as possible, and to have people around me who are not frightened by this transition and can support me in letting go."

D. Who are the people you would like to say good-bye to and thank for what they've added to your life? Write down the mementos you would like to give to individuals. What truth telling would you still like to do before you go?

E. Rehearse your final moments. Where would you like to be? Who would you like to be present, or would you wish to be alone? Is there any music, poetry, or inspirational texts you'd like to hear?

F. Write your own obituary. Are there things in your ideal obituary that you haven't completed yet? On a separate page, write, in the voice of your children or friends, how they remember you. In what way are the two writings different? How are they similar?

G. Hold your memorial service while you're alive. Gather the people with whom you feel closest. First, tell each person what he or she means to you, what each has given you and what you love about them. Take your time, giving all those present their due and savoring the qualities as you express them.

Then close your eyes and invite people to come up behind you, put their hands on your shoulders, and tell you what they love about you. Don't respond or speak, just receive—the words, the touch, the feelings. Notice the themes in what you love in others, and the qualities they love in you. Give thanks for the abundance of love. Hallelujah.

Glossary

Baal Shem Tov — Means "Master of the Good Name" and refers to Rabbi Israel ben Eliezer, who founded Hasidism in the eighteenth century.

Chabad — Worldwide Hasidic movement, a branch of Orthodox Judaism, which has its headquarters in Brooklyn, New York. Members of Chabad are also known as Lubavitcher.

cholent — A stew of meat, potatoes, beans, and barley, traditionally prepared before Shabbat and kept warm in a low oven to conform with Jewish laws that prohibit cooking on the Sabbath.

chuppah — The traditional wedding canopy.

chutzpah — Audacity or brazen nerve.

daven — To pray. When Orthodox Jews daven, they recite the Hebrew words in a singsong pattern, bending forward rhythmically at the waist.

Gan Eden — The Garden of Eden.

goy (pl. *goyim*, adj. *goyishe*) — A person who's not Jewish.

hametz — Any food made of grain that's been fermented and allowed to rise, such as bread, cake, or cookies. Jews are forbidden to eat *hametz* during Passover. Instead, they eat matzah, unleavened bread, to remind themselves of the exodus from Egypt, when the Jews couldn't wait for bread to rise.

Hasid (pl. Hasidim) — A member of the Hasidic movement, which emphasizes devotion and union with God through prayer, song, and strict observance of the laws. There are numerous Hasidic groups and dynasties, including the Lubavitcher, or Chabad.

Kabbalah — Set of esoteric teachings, the mystic branch of Judaism.

Kaddish — The mourners' prayer.

karass — A word coined by Kurt Vonnegut in *Cat's Cradle*, meaning a group of people who work together, sometimes unknowingly, to do God's work.

kohen — Priest, a member of the priestly class that's believed to be descended from Moses's brother Aaron.

kosher — Food that may be consumed according to Jewish law, or anything approved or sanctified for use.

kvetch — Yiddish for "complain."

l'chaim — A toast that means "to life."

Lubavitch or Lubavitcher — Someone who belongs to the Lubavitch sect, or Chabad. Lubavitch and Chabad are used interchangeably.

Lubavitcher Rebbe — Leader of Chabad or the Lubavitch sect.

Mazel tov — "Congratulations!" or "good luck."

mensch — A Yiddish word that roughly means "a good person, a stand-up guy, a person of integrity, possessing the qualities one would hope for in a friend or trusted colleague."

meshugge — Yiddish for "crazy."

mezuzah — Small parchment scroll enclosed in a case that is fixed to the doorframe of Jewish homes. The scroll contains the Shema prayer, which affirms God's oneness and commands Jews to inscribe the words on the doorposts of their homes.

mikvah — A ritual bath in which people immerse themselves to gain purity.

minyan — Quorum of ten men required for a prayer service. In progressive Judaism, women are counted in the minyan.

Mishnah — The first printed record of oral interpretations of the Torah and Jewish laws, compiled about 200 AD.

mitzvah — One of the 613 commandments given in the Torah. Also means a good deed or act of kindness.

nigun — A wordless melody intended to lift the soul.

Nu — A Yiddish interjection meaning "well" or "so?"

payos — Long curly sidelocks worn by Orthodox men, to satisfy the Biblical injunction against shaving the "corners" of the head.

Rebbe or Reb — Yiddish for "Rabbi."

Ruach HaKodesh — The Holy Spirit, from the Hebrew words for "holy breath."

schmatta — Yiddish for a "rag," "junk," or "cheap garment."

seder — Ritual feast that marks the beginning of Passover.

Shabbat — Hebrew for "Sabbath," the day of rest, beginning at sundown Friday night and ending at sundown Saturday. The Orthodox and Yiddish speakers, including Reb Zalman, pronounce it "Shabbos." Other denominations and Israelis say "Shabbat."

shadchan — Hebrew for "matchmaker."

Shakti — Sanskrit term for "the divine feminine creative power."

Shema — Considered the centerpiece of Jewish prayer services. Traditionally, Jews aim to recite the Shema as their last words: "Hear, O Israel: the Lord is our God, the Lord is One."

shochet — Ritual slaughterer who ensures that animals are killed with compassion and respect.

shtetl — A small, poor village of Jews, mostly Yiddish-speaking, located in many areas of Eastern Europe before World War II.

shul — Yiddish for "synagogue" or "prayer house."

smicha — Rabbinic ordination, or transmission of rabbinic authority.

tahara — Purification, the ritual washing of the body after someone has died, done in preparation for burial.

tallith — Prayer shawl.

Talmud — A key text of Judaism containing the opinions and interpretations of thousands of rabbis over the centuries, on topics ranging from law and ethics to history and the Hebrew bible.

tefillin — Two small black leather boxes containing parchment scrolls inscribed with verses from the Torah. When praying, Orthodox men wear them on the forehead and one arm, held in place by leather straps.

teshuva — Repentance, or returning to the path of moral rightness.

tikkun olam — Repairing or healing the world. Judaism teaches that each person is responsible for doing his or her part to heal the world.

Torah — Specifically refers to the first five books of Moses in the Bible, but is used more generally to mean the totality of Jewish teaching and practice.

traif — Not kosher, unclean.

tzadik (pl. *tzadikim*) — A righteous or holy person.

tzitzit — Long narrow fringes attached to an undergarment worn by Orthodox men, to remind them to obey God's commandments.

yarmulke — Round skull cap worn by orthodox men, and by women and men in progressive synagogues, to remind them God is above.

yeshiva — Jewish school that focuses on the study of religious texts.

Yom Kippur — Day of Atonement, one of the two High Holidays, on which people take stock and repent.